Indigenous Knowledge and Resource Management

Indigenous Knowledge and Resource Management

Perspectives of a Tribe in Northeast India

Jumyir Basar

Maulana Abul Kalam Azad Institute of Asian Studies, Kolkata

Anshah Publishing House

ISBN: 978-81-8364-097-8

First Published in India in 2014

Indigenous Knowledge and Resource Management: Perspectives of a Tribe in Northeast India

Published by:
ANSHAH PUBLISHING HOUSE
LG 18-19, Pankaj Central Market, I.P. Ext.,
Patparganj, Delhi-110092, Tel: 22235152, 9810522367
Br.Off. 4617/18, Ansari Road, Darya Ganj,
New Delhi-110002, Tel: 9650028065

Preface

One of the major areas of research that has kept the researchers, academics, planners, activists engaged is issues pertaining to development of people. In fact research interest in this topic has emerged in both disciplinary and interdisciplinary perspectives. It is to be mentioned that the issue of development and research interest have its origin, as many scholars believe, in the inaugural speech of Harry S. Truman, the President of USA, which he delivered on the occasion of taking the office on 20 January 1949. In his speech he used the terms like 'underdevelopment' and 'underdeveloped area' and advocated extending the benefits of scientific advances and industrial progress of USA for the improvement and growth of underdeveloped areas. Since then many policies have been enacted, strategies formulated and programmes launched to develop the underdeveloped areas. Interestingly, the strategies adopted do not prove effective to achieve the development goals and so the strategies have been kept on changing. In these changing experiments with development strategies some times one or the other social factors get importance while in other times these are ignored.

Ignorance to culture in general and IKS in particular during earlier experiments with development and their significance in present development discourse is a case to the point. Considering the shifting and changing nature of the strategies and significance to a factor in development model a natural question arises how long IKS will influence the development perspective and how long IKS will retain its characteristics when it is linked to market propelled development that promotes individualism. This question was the basis of formulation of the research project entitled *A Study of Indigenous Knowledge System and Resource Management Practice among the Galo Tribe of Arunachal Pradesh*. The project was funded by Maulana Abul Kalam Azad Institute of Asian Studies, (MAKAIAS), Kolkata. The present volume is the outcome of the data collected for the project work and the encouragement from MAKAIAS to publish the report.

Needless to say, I am immensely grateful to MAKAIAS, Kolkata for funding the project and undertaking its publication. In addition, the preparation of this volume owes my gratitude to many. It would be fitness of the things to record my highest sense of gratitude and recognition for the help and cooperation I received from the villagers of the study villages during my field study.

I acknowledge my deep sense of gratitude to Prof. David R. Syiemlieh, former Vice Chancellor, Rajiv Gandhi University and Prof. Tamo Mibang, present Vice Chancellor, Rajiv Gandhi University and former Director, Arunachal Institute of Tribal Studies (AITS) who always provide an academic platform and encourage academic pursuits in no uncertain terms.

I also owe my thanks to Ms. Devi Baruah, Assistant Professor, Department of Commerce, Rajiv Gandhi University who went through the manuscript and pointed out the lapses.

Preparation of this MSS for publication within a short time could never have been possible without the help and support of my family members. I am thankful to my father-in-law Shri Dagjom Loyi and mother-in-law Smti. Bade Loyi for their encouragement in all possible ways. My parents, Dr. Tajum Basar and Smti. Dakter Basar, always remains my source of inspirations for all academic pursuits. I am thankful to them for all the support and care they have taken towards my education. I am also thankful to my husband Dr. Jommi Loyi, who has whole heartedly supported me in all my endeavours.

Last but not least, I am thankful to MAKAIAS, Kolkata and for undertaking the publication work and bringing out the book in time.

Jumyir Basar

Contents

List of Appendix and Charts

List of Appendix

List of Charts

List of Plates

Abbreviations

AOP	:	Annual Operating Plan
APHIL	:	Arunachal Horticulture Processing Industries Limited
APO	:	Assistant Political Officer
ARF	:	Anchal Reserve Forests
CBD	:	Convention on Biological Diversity
CD	:	Community Development
CPR	:	Common Property Resources
DDT	:	Dichlorodiphenyltrichloroethane
FAO	:	Food and Agriculture Organisation
FFDA	:	Fish Farmers Development Agency
GoAP	:	Government of Arunachal Pradesh
GOI	:	Government of India
GoN	:	Government of Nagaland
HDR	:	Human Development Report
HYV	:	High Yielding Variety
ICAR	:	Indian Council for Agricultural Research
IKS	:	Indigenous Knowledge System
ILO	:	International Labour Organisation
ITK	:	Indigenous Technical Knowledge
IUCN	:	International Union for Conservation of Nature
JFM	:	Joint Forestry Management
MIP	:	Minor Irrigation Projects
MP	:	Member of Parliament
MT	:	Metric Tonnes
nd	:	Not Dated
NEFA	:	North East Frontier Agency

NEICSSR	:	North-East India Council for Social Science Research
NGO	:	Non Governmental Organisation
NRI	:	Non Resident Indian
PIC	:	Prior Information Consent
PRA	:	Participatory Rural Appraisal
RCC	:	Reinforced Cement Concrete
SGSY	:	Swaranjayanti Gram Swarojgar Yojana
TRC	:	Terrace Rice Cultivation
UNESCO	:	United Nations Educational, Scientific and Cultural Organisation
UNO	:	United Nations Organisation
USF	:	UN-classed State Forests
VLW	:	Village Level Worker
WRC	:	Wet Rice Cultivation
WSSD	:	World Summit on Sustainable Development

I

Introduction

There is a growing recognition to the importance of IKS as a strategy in sustainable and participatory development right from 1980s. This recognition has been further endorsed in the Brundtland Commission Report (1987), IUCN (1980), FAO (1991), WSSD (2002); UNESCO (2002), World Bank (1997) and ILO (1957 & 1989). An aspect of this strategy also recognizes tribal practice of harmonious resource use. The Draft National Tribal Policy 2006 mentions that "The tribal communities' entire way of life is woven around harmony with the preservation of nature. There is a very strong symbolic relationship between the STs and the forests and they have been at the forefront of the conservation regime". This relationship is coined as 'giving environment' by Bird-David (1990, 1992). In fact, this understanding of the relationship between IKS and resource management has been translated into development schemes by Nagaland Government (GoN, 1980) and also through different schemes of G.B. Pant Institute of Himalayan Environment and Development. (see Sundriyal and Jamir, 1999).

But this harmonious relationship, as mentioned, is compatible with the subsistence mode of livelihood which the tribal community practised earlier. Presently, these communities no longer practise subsistence economy as they have been integrated to the market economy through the process of development interventions. Almost all the tribal communities are in the process of transition. (Desai, 1969/ 1992). The process of transition has established a new relationship between the tribes and their environment. In many cases they do not use the resources for their subsistence needs. Moreover, the resources are being put into different and a number of uses during the transitional phase. Besides, the resources from tribal areas find their use beyond tribal communities. There are instances where emerging tribal elites appropriate community resources for commercial purposes. They do so by misinterpreting customary practices. (Behera, 1994: 346).

Land is no more used for shifting cultivation to meet subsistence food requirements. Land is also being put into permanent wet rice cultivation to meet the market needs. Usually, efforts are made to produce more for the market also. The need of the tribe has been diversified; so also the demand for consumer goods. Experience shows that tribal households without any jobs depend on their resources as sources of income.

However, the relation of the tribes with indigenous knowledge cannot be undermined in contemporary period. The tribes in general and tribes living in hills particular still use IK in their economic pursuits. This situation is more visible among hill tribes of Northeast India, most of whom are linked to general plan programmes. (GoI, 1986-87: 36). Nevertheless, they still have anchoring on their traditions and knowledge systems. Though they participate in development process, there has emerged inter and intra tribal variation in this regard. Among Northeast tribes Arunachal tribes have a different status in development process. This is because development initiatives begun with a well defined policy framework of Nehru and Elwin, popularly known as tribal *panchsheel* (Nehru, 1959: xiii), which in essence has bearing on the significance on the people's knowledge. The tribal *panchsheel* reads:

i) "People should develop along the lines of their own genius and we should avoid imposing anything on them. We should try to encourage in every way their own tradition, arts and culture.
ii) Tribal rights on land and forests should be respected.

iii) We should try to train and build up a team of their own people to do the work of administration and development. Some technical personnel from outside will, no doubt, be needed, especially in the beginning. But we should avoid introducing too many outsiders into tribal territory.

iv) We should not over-administer these areas or overwhelm them with multiplicity of schemes. We should rather work through, and not in rivalry to, their own social and cultural institutions.

v) We should judge results, not by statistics or the amount of money spent, but by the quality of human character that is evolved". (Nehru, ibid).

Under such changing situations the present piece of research work explores the status of IKS in resource management, precisely the connections between the two, with Galo tribe of Arunachal Pradesh as case study.

The Galo

The Galo is one of the tribes of Arunachal Pradesh, which earlier was considered as a sub-tribe/group of the Adi tribe. Their reference is found in various Assamese chronicles by the name *Abor*, a term used to refer to the earlier Adi group (see Nyori, 1993:3). The colonial writers adopted the term *Abor* but in many of their writings different terminologies have been used to refer to different groups of Adi. For example, the Padams have been mentioned as Bor Abors, the Minyongs as Meyong Abors, and the Galos as Dhobas/Dubba Abors (*c.f* Mackenzie, 1994:36). Like the other *Tani* groups, they trace their origin to *Abo Tani*[1], the mythical forefather. The Galos are mainly distributed in three districts of the state namely, West Siang, East Siang and Upper Subansiri with maximum concentration in West Siang District. They reside in Dumporijo and Baririjo circles of Upper Subansiri and in Nari, New Seren, Kora and Koyu circles of East Siang districts.

Racially the Galos belong to the Mongoloid stock.

Linguistically they belong to the North Assam group of Tibeto-Burman languages. The total population of the Galo is not available as in the 2011 census there has been no tribe wise enumeration and classification. However, Riba (2009) has enumerated population of Galo inhabited villages fully and partially in three districts. He has based his enumeration on the basis of census 2001 and field survey conducted during the period from 2004-2008. As per his information in Upper Subansiri district there are 66 Galo habitations, including villages and administrative headquarters, with a total population of 9643. In West Siang district he has enumerated 258 habitations, villages, administrative centres and camp settlements with a population of 71,941. In East Siang district he has recorded 31 such habitations with a population of 6172. The total population in Galo villages in three districts comes to 87,756. Of course, there are a few villages with mixed population but their population is not very significant. It is to be further mentioned that there are Galo settlements in Lohit, Changlang, Itanagar and in Lower Dibang Valley districts. So it can be stated with certainty that the Galo population in total cannot be less than the total population figure given for the three districts.

In the absence of any specific study, it would not be exaggeration to state that on the basis of observation the Galos are one of very few tribes, others being the Apatanis and the Adis, who have been better integrated in the process of development. It is worth mentioning that a number of executive posts in the state like a two former Chief Secretaries, the former Director of Higher Education and two former Directors of Health Services were members of Galo community. Similarly, there are pioneers in other fields like the medical specialist, Ph.D degree holder in nuclear physics, law degree holder, film production, etc. The first M.P. to Rajya Sabha, the first NRI, the first Chairperson in the State Commission for Women, the first Arunachalee to hold the post of Controller of Examinations in the lone university in the State are from this community. This shows that the Galos have accepted the modern development process[2] which is different from their traditional life of harmony with the nature. Added to it, the primary investigator herself belongs to the Galo community and therefore has the advantage of communication in a common lingua franca, i.e. Galo. That is why the tribe has been selected for the present study.

Review of Literature

There are enough works relating to IKS and sustainable resource use. There are some studies which advocate integration of the Indigenous people and their knowledge to world development in political, economic and other spheres. A few of such works have been reviewed. In the works by Satapathy (1997), Barik (1998, 2004), Rai and Maharana (2004), Saikia and Das (2004) there is a stress on IKS in sustainable development strategies. In the works of Borang (1997) and Ramakrishnan (1997) the sustainable resource use practices by traditional communities have been described. Ramakrishnan finds traditional systems in north east context often energy efficient with high economic returns to the farmers.

Gadgil and Guha (1992) have discussed human-nature relationship in historical perspective within a unifying framework of four themes namely; prudence, profligacy, strategies of resource use, and the conflicts which they give rise to. They have located the restraining practices of resource use in specific cultural and historical contexts in India. Precisely, they have presented a new interpretation of emergence of cultural and ecological mosaic of Indian society and a socio-ecological analysis of the emerging modes of resource use and consequent conflicts during British period. Theoretically, the authors have forwarded an analytical scheme, i.e. 'modes of resource use', to supplement to the concept of 'mode of production' for broad historical periodisation of human-natural resource relationship. The authors (1995) in another work have presented the contemporary conflicts in resource use in the process of development. They have argued for a new environment friendly agenda for development in which the focus should be on sustainable use of India's environmental resources, particularly the forest resources, in the interest of the masses. There is a strong appeal for people's involvement and implicitly the focus is on people's knowledge. Taking the argument of sustainable resource use a little further, Guha (2008) questions the relevance of large scale resource consumption in the West and attributes resource conflicts, and regulated regime in resource use, planning, management and conservation strategies in non-western societies to the higher and growing level of consumption requirements in the West.

There are few works which have essentially ecological focus while explaining shifting cultivation in Northeast India (Danda, 1994; ICAR, 1983; NEICSSR, 1976/1980). Ramakrishnan (1993) has made a scientific study of IK related to traditional *jhum* practices in Northeast India, which to him, are often energy efficient, and at the same time provide high economic returns to the farmers. Perhaps this could be the reason for which shifting cultivation is continuing inspite of the fact that government policies and schemes have been enacted to discourage the practice. In this regard Mili, Dollo, Samal and Singh (2010) suggest, drawing on field data, for the scientific management of the shifting cultivation without discarding it. Works with focus on shifting cultivation (Behera, 2004; Borang 1998), changing human-nature relationship (Behera and Mantaw, 1997; Behera 2008; Behera 2010) and traditional resource use practices (Ramakrishnan, 1997 & Singh, 1997) in Arunachal Pradesh are also available. Gyati (2005) has discussed the uses of common property resources in biodiversity and water conservation, and in forestry among the Apatanis. She has focused on the inhibitions in the use of common property resources (CPR) in general and performance of natural resource linked rituals in particular in response to policy interventions through Wild Life Protection Act, JFM, and the National Biodiversity Strategies and Action Plans.

On Galo there are three ethnographic works which have focused on some aspects of IKS in resource management. Behera (1998-99) in a village study has made some passing references to some indigenous beliefs and practices applied by

Galo women in orange cultivation. Riba (1998) has discussed the agricultural transformation in Galo community and he (2000) has also worked on the changing relationships between human and environment with reference to changing physical and cultural environment of the area inhabited by the Galo. He has particularly identified some aspects of IKS with focus on ITK applied by the Galo especially in fishing. (See Riba, 1997 & 2003. Chaudhuri et al (2008) have discussed indigenous fishing and preservation techniques, conservation practices, ownership of fishing sources, various uses of fishes and other aspects of cultural significance of fish in Adi, Galo and Nyishi communities of Arunachal Pradesh. They have also made references to changes in traditional practices. The aim of their study has conservation policy at the core. Basar (2004) has presented an ethnographic study of resource and resource management in village Nyigam in relation to economic pursuits of the people. In a similar line, though implicit, Gibi (2004) and Riba (2004) have discussed resource use pertaining to economic pursuits in Tatamori and Dari villages in West Saing district respectively. Riba (2004 a) has described indigenous knowledge in the form of traditional social capital as used by Galo in house construction with Dishi village of West Siang district as case study. In another study Riba (1998a) has described the ritualistic relationship between human and tiger.

Other works on Galo mainly deal with their socio cultural life. Earlier works on Galo (who were mentioned in various names such as Doba, Abors, Galongs or Gallongs, Ghasi Miris) were accounts on their life-style left by administrative officers (Dalton, 1872; Dunn, 1896; Annual Reports, 1905-6, 1906-7, etc.). Perhaps, the account of the people as Galongs appeared first time in 1913 in the Journal of the Asiatic Society of Bengal (Dunbar, 1915). During the same time they figured in the same name in the sketch map showing tribes on the north-east frontier. (see Shakespeare, 1914).

Verrier Elwin has presented a general account of the Galos, aspects of their socio-cultural life (1959), myths and legends (1958) and of material culture (1959(a)). Srivastava (1962) has given a preliminary idea about the people and their land, their material culture, social and economic organization, rituals and beliefs and few other related aspects of their life style. Dasgupta (1963) has studied about their language. In the field of language of the Galo the contribution of Post (2007, 2008 & 2010), a linguist, needs a mention though his works were not reviewed because of their technical nature.

Sarkar (1987), Lal and Dasgupta (1979), Dasgupta (1987) and Behera (1999) have thrown light on practices related to Galo marriage system. Bhattacharjee (1993) has presented an account of his experience with Galo people in 1960s. Dutta (1976) gives an account of their Mopin festival. Norbu (1997) has described the status of Galo women with reference to sex based division of labour, recreation and participation in socio-cultural activities. On socio-economic conditions, Dutta and Duarah (1965), Goswami and Saikia (1971) and Dutta (1997) have provided some general accounts.

There are works by Galo scholars relating to culture in general. Nyori (1993) has focused on various aspects of life style of the Galo as a sub-tribe of the Adi. He (1998) has also described the faiths and practices of his people from an insider point of view. Ete, (1983/1984, 1985) has documented Galo folklores and has translated a few of them in English. Lollen (2004) has traced the growth of Kombo village through legends and historical antecedents. In two other works (2006 & 2007) he has studied symbolism in Galo marriage rituals and proverbs. Quite a good number of studies (Potom (2006); Riba (2006); Basar (2006, 2007); Doji (2006) & Karbak (2006, 2007); Karlo (2007)) are available focusing on various aspects of marriage systems like rituals and taboos, exchanges, *aben kabnam*[3], legends, entertainments etc. of the people under study. Preliminary inquiries have also been made on topics pertaining to changes in agriculture (Eshi, 1998), social institutions (Loyi, 2001), some aspects of culture in general (Bagra, 2002), linkage with forest (Gamlin, 2002), customary laws (Kakki, 2004), Mopin festival (Riba, 2006 (a)), and on fertility and mortality (Koyu, 2009). Bagra (2009) has analysed Galo folklores to understand women as 'others'. Karlo (2005) has studied the changing pattern of grassroots leadership in Galo community-both traditional and emerging- in terms of its determinants, attitudes and perceptions along with the decision making process in the context of rapid democratic decentralisation.

Significance and Policy Implications

The significance of the study of IKS in resource management stems from the realisation to link environment with development programme in the era of globalisation. The IKS being culture specific and globalisation having homogenising tendency the study provides an insight into the understanding of integration of local specificity in the homogenising force of globality[4].

The tribal communities in general and the Galo in particular are in transition. During the transitional phase the resource use in tribal communities is linked to market forces. But in traditional communities due to the absence of market forces and with subsistence livelihoods strategy the human-nature relationship happens to be harmonious. Contrarily, the present model of development with predominant market forces the relation of development is not environmental friendly. It is therefore imperative to know if the emphasis on IKS in resource management has a standing in the transitional phase of development guided by market forces. Precisely, the research attempts at exploring the status of IKS in a changing context. Herein lies the importance of this present study.

Essentially, the study has both theoretical and empirical groundings. The relation between IKS in resource management and sustainable development in a theoretical sense is empirically verified with Galo tribe as case study. Undoubtedly, it adds to the existing knowledge in the field.

The scope of the study has both practical and policy implications. It is believed to disseminate the knowledge in the field among the development practitioners in general and people in particular.

Objectives

The main objectives of the study are as follows:

i) to list the resources and their changing uses by the Galos;
ii) to study faiths, belief, practices and taboos associated with resource management;
iii) to examine the status of IKS and study the harmony between human-nature relationship in the changing context;
iv) to study the extent of resource use consequent upon development interventions;
v) to record if there is any conflict between the government and the community in resource use; and
vi) to make suggestions for formulation of sustainable development strategies by incorporating IKS.

Methodology

The present study is empirical in nature and descriptive in analysis. Data for analysis have been collected from both primary and secondary sources. The secondary source consists of relevant books, journals, periodicals, audio-visual documentations of NGOs and Government Departments at the state as well as district level, such as Department of Economics and Statistics, Directorates of Rural Development, Agriculture, Horticulture, Fisheries, Forests, etc. For a deeper understanding of the socio-culture life of the people related works have been consulted not only from published books but also from archive records.

The study is essentially diachronic in nature. The contemporary human-nature relationship is juxtaposed with that of the past period of reference which is defined as the time period before the development interventions, roughly before 1947.

Primary data have been collected from field study. Data on traditional human-nature relationship have also been collected from folk-lores with reference to the worldview of the community in general. Myths, legends and folk tales, life histories, etc. have been collected for the purpose.

During field study, simple anthropological methods and

techniques like observation, case studies and interview have been used. PRA methods and techniques have been applied to capture the ground reality of the research problem. Internal records of the line departments have also been consulted. Both formal and informal discussions have been conducted with development functionaries at village, block, district and state levels.

In this study, as is evident, the Galo community living in three districts of Arunachal Pradesh constitutes the universe. The villages and knowledgeable persons have provided the sample frame. Of the total Galo villages in these three districts twenty five villages were proposed for the study. have been purposively selected for sample purpose keeping the distance from district headquarters in view.

In East Siang District the Galo inhabits two CD Blocks, namely Koyu and Nari. In Koyu CD Block there are two circles namely Koyu and Kora. In these two circles there are 14 villages. Out of these fourteen villages there are villages like Sido with mixed population; the Galos and Adis settle together in such villages. Villages in Nari and New Seren Circles are located in plains. There are 16 villages out of which Depi, Depi Moli, Detak are mixed with Adi tribes. The villages in Nari and New Seren Circles have been using land for WRC before the plan interventions. The resource use in these villages is much more influenced by the pattern of resource use prevailing in adjacent villages of Assam. From the villages in Nari CD Block there are some camps with mixed population. In total Riba (2009) has enumerated 31 settlements, a majority with total Galo population and a few with mixed population, which comes, as mentioned earlier, to 6172.

In Upper Subansiri the Galo villages are found in Dumporijo and Baririjo Circles. There are in total 66 Galo settlements with a population of 9643. (Riba, ibid). During the pilot survey it was found that 36 villages have households between 3 and 12. In some of these villages terrace cultivation is found; but the WRC fields are very few. Shifting cultivation in predominant. The resource use pattern is similar to those of the Tagin villages because all these villages avail schemes from the same district administration. Similar is the case in East Siang district. That is why quantitative information relating to resource use in the Galo villages of Upper Subansiri and East Siang District were not available for Galo people separately, as they are mixed with other tribal groups.

The pilot survey presented a much diverse picture in three Galo inhabited district as far as changing resource use pattern is concerned. The diversity as it was understood has resulted from the difference in administration of three different districts. Every district has its own commitment to the welfare of its people. But as it was understood during field study generally the minor groups are neglected. This idea was also given by the people in sample villages as Galo villages are in minority in Upper Subansiri and East Siang districts. It is but natural to think that the attention of district administration has more focus on major groups. But it is not the case in West Siang district. Except a few pockets it is entirely dominated by Galo population. Riba (ibid) has enumerated 258 Galo habitations with a population of 71,941 as recorded earlier.

It is to be mentioned that the researcher did not have the time or adequate resource to verify whether people's views about the negligence of minor communities by the administration is correct or not. That is why intensive field work was conducted in 16 villages of West Siang district keeping in view the topical interest of the present work.

Nevertheless, the field study was conducted in Telam, Old Seren, Nari and Koyu villages of East Siang District. Similarly, field study was conducted in Belo, Beyar, Ronya, Hyder and Digbak villages of Upper Subansiri district. The purpose was to collect qualitative information on traditional resource use practice so as to understand the resource use by the Galo in a general perspective. The 16 villages in West Siang district are selected considering most exposed (Category I), moderately exposed (Category II) and less exposed (Category III) criteria on the basis of developmental indices like road communication, literacy, occupational diversity, availability of amenities like school, electricity, water supply; commercial activities like horticulture garden, tea plantation, proximity to urban/

business centres, etc. There are 4 villages (Tadin, Paya, Darka and Kabu) selected from the more exposed group, 3 villages (Ratak Gamlin, Chekor Lombi and Liru) from moderately exposed group and 9 villages (Belo, Yiga, Tapo, Piri, Siru, Lite Boje, Siru Tali, Ringi and Bogo) from the less exposed one.

To understand the Galo worldview in general and human-nature relationship in particular, 15 *nyibo*s (shamans) and *nyikoks* (knowledgeable persons other than *nyibos*) from the entire Galo area have been interviewed.

As has been mentioned, the researcher is herself a Galo and so has the advantage of easy communication with the Galo respondents. But, being an insider has also its own limitations. The investigator is conscious of the limitations what in research parlance is known as emic biases. In this regard it is to be mentioned that the researcher is trained in the discipline of anthropology, and so she has a mind set to understand the issues relating to the topic of research critically and objectively. Anthropologists have recognised that "... the importance of training in formal anthropological research ...should help one to overcome the subjective bias" (Madan, 1986/2004, p. 198; also see Mibang and Behera, 2004, pp. 6-12; Berreman, 1968/2004, pp. 157-190).

The research was completed within a period of two years. During the first six months pilot study was carried out. On the basis of the information collected from the pilot study, sample villages were selected and schedules constructed. Knowledgeable persons, both traditional and modern were identified and contact established for interview. This took another six months. In the next six months relevant literature, government records and archival records were collected and consulted. However, consultation of literature continued during the entire research work whenever it was possible.

The last 12 months were devoted to the field study, data transcription and analysis and report writing.

Chapterisation

The study is organized into the following six chapters:

Chapter I: Introduction

This chapter includes: a brief introduction to the research issue, review of literature, objectives, methodology, significance and policy implications, and chapterisation. It also presents a brief profile of the Galos.

Chapter II: Contours of Resource Use

This chapter identifies the type of resources and the purpose for which these resources are used by the Galo people. In addition to this the chapter also describes social, economic, political and cultural contexts of resource use. Moreover, the concept of resource in Galo community has been discussed from people's perspective.

Chapter III: Galo World-view and Resource Use

In this chapter the focus is on utilisation, preservation and conservation of natural resources within the frame of worldview of the Galo people. The relation between natural resources, namely, land, forests and water, and the Galos have been described with reference to their faiths and beliefs.

Chapter IV: Indigenous Technical Knowledge in Resource Use: Changing Perspectives

The chapter discusses the technical knowledge system of the people which they employ in their day-to-day life in the process of resource utilization. Further the chapter also briefly presents the changing perspective in the use of ITK.

Chapter V: Findings and Analysis

The chapter critically examines the contemporary scenario and the process of change in the use of various resources in response to government interventions. It has tried to locate traditional ethics and values in the sustainable use of these resources.

Chapter VI: Summary and Conclusions

The discussions in the foregoing chapters have been summarized and suggestions having policy implications forwarded for formulation of development strategies pertaining to resource use more objectively.

NOTES

1. *Tani* is the name of the forefather. He is also believed to be the first human being from whom the human race evolved. *Abo* means father. It is a tradition among the *Tani* group of tribes in general and Galo in particular to address an ancestor or any honourable person as *Abo* (father), *Ane* (mother), *Achi* (elder brother), *Anyi* (elder sister), etc. either prefixed or suffixed. The people address *Tani* as *Abo Tani*.
2. See Commoner, 1971 for an understanding of the link between the development process using modern technology and environmental degradation.
3. *Aben kabnam* is a ritualistic song which normally explains the reason of happenings pertaining to social phenomenon/institution/relation in Galo community. But in marriage it reasons out such practices as the origin of marriage, girls going to husband's house after marriage, sacrifice of mithun, etc. Besides the bride also seeks blessings through *aben* at the time of departure.
4. This is related to the debate between globalisation and glocalisation. (Khondker, 2004; also see Behera, 2009: 3-35, for universalising globalisation through local specificity). That the globalisation has homogenising effect through integration at different levels is evident from the following quote, "Globalization expands the opportunities for unprecedented human advance for some but shrinks those opportunities for others and erodes human security. It is integrating economy, culture and governance but fragmenting societies". (UNDP, 1999: 43).

II

Contours of Resource Use

The Galos primarily use land, water and forests available in their neighbourhoods for their material means of existence. These are natural resources. They also depend on domesticated animals and birds as livelihood options. But in this chapter only natural resources have been discussed.

The Galo Perception of Resource

The Galos have a common classificatory term *Gida-isi,* meaning land and forest *(Gida)* or *Kode-isi*[1], meaning land (*Kode*) and water (*isi*) to designate all the natural sources from which they draw their material needs. Normally, *kode-isi* includes land, water and forests in a usufructuary sense at individual level. On various occasions the Galos enquire about *kode-isi*. For example, during marriage the bride party enquires if the groom family has *kode-isi* or not – *Kode-isi kan goru ye?* Similarly, when someone refers to the resource base of a village s/he enquires whether the *kode-isi* of the village of reference is good or bad- *Dolu kode-isi e al doye?* In the former case *Kode-isi* which includes generally land and water has an ownership dimension while in the later it refers to quality of land in forest and water in the village.

Kode has both general and specific meanings. In general sense it includes both land and forests. In its specific meaning *kode* refers to land, particularly to soil, and is distinguished from the forests which are called *motum.* The Galos use the term *motum* to designate all types of forests.

It should be mentioned that each and every landscape which the Galos use, or know about, has a name of its own. Similarly, different forests have different names[2]. So what the Galos mean by *kode-isi* includes three natural resources namely- land (*Kode*), forests (*motum*) and water (*isi*). These resources assume significance in terms of their various uses to which Galos put them to fulfil their material needs in a culturally defined way. Evidently, resources have their significance as a means of fulfilling material desires of Galo people and as reflected in their faiths and beliefs.

Though *motum* is the general term for forest, it is also perceived from the perspective of and use for cultivation. All the lands are viewed as forests and cultivable land as well. So, *moro* and *mobi,* which are forest categories, are also two different categories of *jhum* fields. Needless to say, people do not make any exclusive distinction between forests and land resources.

Generally, the Galo people use forests for almost all of their material requirements. From various uses we can classify uses of forests by the Galos as follows:

i) collection of forest products as construction materials for residential houses, granaries, bridges, fencing, etc.;
ii) forest lands are reclaimed to prepare *jhum* fields;
iii) use of forest lands for grazing;
iv) collection of ritual items;
v) collection of items like green leaves, fruits, roots, etc. as dietary supplements;
vi) hunting to supplement diets and as ritualistic requirements; and
vii) collection of fuel and medicine.

Resource Use

Resource use is discussed in a broader context including both the use and conservation aspects. Hence, resource management and resource use have been interchangeably used. Resource management roughly means the use of resources for securing material means of existence- food, clothing and shelter. Of course, resource use for curing diseases can be added to the list. But this is not the connotation of what resource management implies in a tribal community like the Galo. As a matter of fact the Galos like other tribal communities use resources in a cultural perspective and hence resource management has a broader connotation than ordinary meaning of resource use to fulfil material needs.

In cultural perspective resource management apparently implies the use of resources as defined in terms of customs, traditions, ethics, values, norms and sanctions. Naturally, resource management in this sense is a holistic perspective through a specialised activity. Therefore, resource management includes use of resources involving human-nature relationship, human-human relationship, and human-nature-supernature relationship. The holistic perspective through a specialised activity is explained in the following paragraph with *jhum* practice as an example.

The resource use in Galo community can broadly be divided into material and non-material categories. The material category includes economic activities, house construction and forest activities. But economic activities with ecosystem people do not form into exclusively a material domain because the material and non material aspects are inter-related and integrated. For example, house construction involves selection of plot through divination and the felling of the trees in *jhum* plots is invariably preceded by ritual performance in the name of spirits dwelling in the trees. However, for convenience of analysis emphasis is given on material aspects in which non-material practices are embodied. Further, depending on the nature of work, the material activity has been purposively divided into economic activity and other material activities. The former includes agriculture, hunting and gathering and handicrafts. Gathering includes such activities as relating to forest and water bodies. The later includes construction works like foot tract, house, granary, etc[3].

Contours of Resource Use

As has been mentioned, resources are used by the Galos for

securing material means of existence. But its rootedness in belief and faiths adds socio-cultural and political dimensions to it. So, resource use has been discussed in its relation to economic, social and political aspects of life.

The socio-cultural dimension of resource use is evident in social occasions like marriage, and religious occasions like festivals and rituals.

The relationship Galos have with their environment is very complex. If we refer to the Galo folktales most of the animals, birds, plants and even leeches can be treated as a kin member, as *Abo Tani* is supposed to have married almost all the living creatures on earth before getting married to *Donyi Mumsi*, the daughter of *Donyi-* the sun.

The resources like agricultural land, river and forest tracts are individual or clan owned but this ownership is in relation to other individuals or clans. In other words, in an individually owned land the others (persons from both within and outside the clan) do not have any use rights without permission. But this ownership is not absolute to the individual owner. Within this individual ownership there are objects like trees, caves, stones, segment of the river or a part of the forest which are believed to have spirits as owners. So the individual ownership of land, forest or river is limited by the extent of the ownership of the spirits within it.

Any dispute regarding the ownership is settled in the village *Keba* or in *Bango Keba or* in *Bogum Boka* depending on the fact whether the dispute is inter villager, intra village or involving the whole tribe. Herein lies the political dimension of resource use in the Galo community.

As has been mentioned, the *Keba*, i.e. village council, plays an important role in administering the resource use practices[4]. Infact, it puts restraints on resource use that violates cultural prescriptions. Any dispute relating to ownership, rent, etc. is settled by the *Keba*. Usually, the dispute arises when there is encroachment upon resources, or when resource is used without permission, or there arises confusion in the ownership or boundary demarcation. The *Keba* prevents the use of common property resource of the village by members other than the concerned village community without proper permission. It protects the ownership rights of individuals and the community over the resources which are encroached upon by those who do not have much resource or use more than their requirements. Use of forest resources, even if these are community-owned, is restricted by rituals and taboos and any violation of it comes under *Keba's* scrutiny. For example, movement taboo is observed at family level or community level after some rituals. As a result, activities relating to resource use are not undertaken. Because of the existence of *Keba* resource use is governed by cultural prescriptions which do not encourage resource use beyond subsistence. Evidently, *Keba's* involvement in resource management is negligible, but given the resource use for subsistence requirement of the community, its role has greater contextual significance.

In the following paragraphs, the use of natural resources such as land, water and forests has been discussed in a broader context relating to economic, social and political dimensions.

Land

The Galos use land for cultivation which is one of their important economic pursuits. *Jhum* lands are individually owned and can be cultivated by others, who are infact members from the Galo community, on lease by paying rent, *patak,* in terms of household articles or domesticated animals like pig or cattle. Now-a-days cash is also used for rent. The researcher could not find any instance of share cropping in any of the sample villages except in *Liru*. In the village of reference the land owners (the Galos) employ non-tribals or other tribal groups like Rabha, Boro, Mishing from neighbouring state of Assam to cultivate the land. The produce is divided into three equal parts- one for the land owner, one for the cultivator and the third as the rent of the land.

The different cultivation practices followed in Galo community are as under:

Modi Rigi/Tump Rike (*jhum* for late variety crops)

This is the main *jhum* field where large scale cultivation is done. It is usually situated at a distance from the river. The seeds are sown in mid-March to May and the crops are harvested during September and October. *Bali, Patu Pama, Pumik, Lite* are the paddy varieties which are sown along with *Tepe* (maize), and *Tami* (millets). Late varieties of paddy are grown in such fields.

Moki Rigi (*jhum* for early variety crops)

This cultivation is practised in fields nearer to the river. Early varieties of paddy like *Kapu, Yayo, Minre* along with maize and millets are cultivated in such fields. The seeds are sown in March and April and harvested in July and August. Such cultivation is usually practised to make available the provision of rice during the lean period before harvesting of the main *jhum* plot or *modi rike.*

Lugo/Lau (Enclosure near house for growing varieties of crops)

Lugo/Lau is practised nearer to the house. Generally, *mede* (variety of paddy) and *peme* (a variety of maize) are grown in *lugo*. Vegetables like *giyi*, *kope*, *bayom* (egg plant), *baki*, *take* (ginger), *yaluk* (chilli) are also grown. The seeds are sown in February and March, and crops are harvested in June and July. This cultivation is practised to meet the food requirement of the family before the main harvest.

Pelek (Maize cultivation)

Generally this cultivation is practised in plots nearer to the river or in land with high moisture content. Mainly *Tepe* (maize) is grown. The subsidiary crops include the tapioca, yam and vegetables. The seeds are sown between November and January and crop is harvested in March and April.

Mali Rigi (Sweet Potato field)

This cultivation is practised after clearing *moro* (dense forest). The production is best when the land is a mixture of soil and small stones (*Liye Lire*). Chilli is also grown along with the *mali*.

Tasak Rigi (Cotton field)

Cotton was grown in plots nearer to the river (*Isi Rui*). Now the Galo people no more cultivate cotton.

Isi Rigi (Wet Rice field)

The practice of wet rice cultivation, including terrace rice cultivation (TRC), has been adopted as a consequence of plan interventions. In this cultivation two varieties of paddy seeds, traditional and non-traditional, are used. The traditional variety has different names in different study villages. In some villages of Basar and Tirbin people remember one variety, called *mipun*, under the traditional variety of paddy. Even in some villages the traditional *dane* variety of paddy is cultivated. In villages of Aalo people call *amo* to a number of traditional varieties. The non-traditional varieties include both high yielding and other paddy varieties adopted from neighbouring non-Galo communities. In the villages of Aalo and Tirbin area these non-traditional varieties of paddy are called *dane* while in Basar area it is called *ai-ret* (probably derived from IR-8, the variety which was introduced initially in the area).

Initially people used to cultivate both traditional and non-traditional varieties. But in the villages of Aalo area people cultivate only dane variety. In other villages both traditional and non-traditional varieties are cultivated, sometimes in combination or as a single variety. In study villages under Basar Circle, a few families cultivate both, while in other villages either *mipun or ai-ret* is cultivated. Generally, the cultivation starts from April-May. Initially when both the varieties were cultivated people either cultivated *mipun* in April-May, followed by dane in June-July or vice-versa. The harvesting season spans from last part of August to early December. It is to be further mentioned that there are differences among the villages with regard to the beginning of sowing and harvesting. This depends on the climatic condition as the Galo villages studied are located in high altitudes with cold climate and plain areas with warm climate.

Associated with the use of land for economic purposes are institutional factors like ownership, inheritance and management. Traditionally, land is mainly used by the Galos for two purposes- cultivation and homestead or the village settlement area. The land may be owned by a community (in terms of village), clan, lineage group or a family. Earlier such ownership was loose as people only claimed rights till they used the land. This was because of their migratory nature. For example, the Ada clan of Tapo village first settled near Basar, then slowly migrated towards Gensi, settling for brief periods at different places and then to present Tapo. They do not claim rights to land they used in course of migration, but as long as they settled in a particular place they enjoyed the usufructuary rights. However, now they have a strong sense of ownership over land and other resources at Tapo and nearby areas.

Inheritance of land is through the male line. Usually the eldest son gets the lion's share. But many a times the distribution of land among the sons depends on the willingness of the father.

Jhum cultivation has been one of the major land use practices from a distant past. Various folklores, myths and tales, are associated with it. Many social occasions are formalised after the main *jhum* activity[5]. For example, the period considered suitable for marriage, festivals and few rituals is just after harvesting and before or during the beginning of the following agricultural season.

The ownership of land resource has a status dimension. The family which cultivated more land had the better social status than the family with less land for cultivation. The family wise inequality in the size of land holdings was not the real inequality per head individual. In the community there was practice of polygyny. A man with more mithuns could marry more than one wife. With more wives in the family the working hands become more and so also the size or number of plots of land cultivated by the family. As a result the number of plots in a family depended on the number of working hands on it. Of course, some of the slave owners had more plots as slaves were also working hands in the family. Obviously, number of working hands and the resultant larger area (more plots) under cultivation was need based rather than having the accumulation tendency.

Sometimes, a family cultivates more number of plots taking into view succeeding year's planning for marriage, house construction or performance of a ritual. The cultivation of more lands requires more working hands which comes from the social process of appropriation of labour through mutual cooperation. Use of land resource is directly related to the family needs and the number of working hands available in the family, thereby putting restraints to use of more land for cultivation. In the absence of accumulation motive there was no class formation in traditional Galo community on the basis of difference in size and pattern of land use.

Mixed cropping and also double cropping are the characteristics of *jhum* cultivation. Though the practice of double cropping in *jhum* has not drawn the attention of the scholars, the present researcher found that after the harvesting of one crop, say paddy, the Galos grow other crops ranging from low quality cereals to root and vegetable crops in the same field. Crops are grown for almost one year in such cases where the field is abandoned after one year's of cultivation. If the field is used for more than one year various types of crops are almost grown together or one after the other continuously for the whole period. This pattern of cropping has provided the 'safety net' for which Galos do not cultivate more land as a precaution against uncertainty.

Forest

Forest is distinguished from the land for the purpose of

analysis as has been mentioned earlier. The Galo people have an intrinsic relationship with the forest which provides them with raw materials essential in their day-to-day life. Hunting is loosely an economic pursuit because it has also ceremonial significance. However, hunting is an economic pursuit in that it is the main source of providing flesh food directly or indirectly through ritual offerings and thus supplement to the dietary intake. In addition to hunting, foraging also forms an important source of dietary supplement. Leaves, fruits, shoots, roots and honey are obtained from the forest which become the main items of food in many families against rainy days.

The social context of forest use relates to organisation of various forest activities. As is the custom in other *Tani* groups of tribes, hunting is exclusively an activity in men's domain. On the other hand, in foraging, both men and women participate, but the nature of involvement of women is regular. Needless to say, the major part of the foraging activity is undertaken by women. The proportion of labour contribution by women is very high.

Hunting is carried out in traditional Galo community either individually or in group. Group hunting or community hunting is termed as *kiruk.* Though there is not much difference between the animals hunted during individual hunting and kiruk, the latter is targeted towards animals like tiger, boar, bear, deer, porcupines, etc. *Kiruk* is organised when there is information about sighting of animals. It is also organised before nyida to feed the groom or bride's family. *Kiruk* is planned in the evening but is organised in the following morning.

In *kiruk* usually kimen (dog) is used as one of the hunting companions. The speciality of kimen is that it can trace out animals through smell. The *kimen* barks and chases the animal with the hunters following it. When an animal is killed, the meat is distributed and the head is given to the hunter as a trophy. In case the kimen kills the animal, its head is given to kimen's master. The head goes to the hunter as per the hunting norms, but all the villagers relish it in the evening with *opo.*

Water

Traditionally, irrigation was not necessary for *jhum* cultivation. In this regard water resource did not have economic use in agriculture. However, river banks provided land types suitable for cultivation of different crops which the Galo used to grow. The water body had also an infrastructural significance as it facilitated transportation during fishing. The Galos used to fish with the help of *esap* (net) and *heyak* from various rafts made of plantain trunks, bamboos, etc. In addition to this indirect economic context, the most significant aspect of water body was that it was an important source of fish food to the Galo people. Usually fishing activity is undertaken during leisure hours.

Being a natural resource, water bodies like rivers passing through a village and natural lakes, streams, streamlets, ponds, etc. are owned by the community. But over the years private ownership has emerged over rivers. Streams, streamlets and other water bodies are not yet individually owned. The ownership of river has changed over the years with two distinct phases. In the first phase, not the whole river segment, but some portions like hile (deep water) are owned. These portions have abundant fish population. In the second phase, in recent times, the whole river is owned in different segments. During first phase the village community could use not only the free portion but also the privately owned segment for fishing.

However, the river is not completely privatised and the social context of fishing still continues. This means that individual members of the village community can fish in any part of the river for self consumption, for which permission is not required. It was reported during field study that individual members while fishing for self consumption also sell the surplus catches if any. The owner of a river segment however fishes for both consumption and sell. But for large scale fishing like *hibok*, the permission of the owner is required. For other purposes like drinking or irrigation permission is not required. As the ownership of other water bodies has not evolved they still remain common property resource. A few of such water bodies are believed to be the abode of yapoms; so they are not usually used for fishing.

Resource use in traditional Galo community had a subsistence dimension. They used the resources to meet their basic needs which were limited in nature. Obviously, the resource use did not have any commercial purpose. It is not surprising that the resources did not have diversified uses and the scale of use was also limited. Further, the use of resources was not a specialised domain of activity; rather it was an institutionalised process embedded in economic, social and political aspects of life.

NOTES

1. *Gida-isi* and *Kode-isi* are synonymous in terms of their meaning. But *Kode-isi* is a popular term frequently used. The use of the term *Gida-isi* has ownership implication.
2. For example, in Piri village, people identify the forests by the names of *Paktir, Jirdi, Pergo, Taben, Dara, Aggo, Yorpek, Tapii-modi, Hiki, Hime, Gayi, Hipo, Yochi, Yotte, Deka, Moya, Yoch, Gune, Morak, Gichi, Gite, Puchi, Pute, Muro, Moko, Danyi Mori, Bensi, Japo* and *Tuker.*
3. For a general understanding of material activity in Galo community, see Srivastava, 1962; Nyori, 1993; Dutta Choudhury, 1994; Norbu, 1997; Eshi, 1998; Behera, 1998-99; Loyi, 2001; Bagra, 2002; Gamlin, 2002; and Riba, 2004 though the studies have been undertaken in different contexts.
4. *C.f. Tatak, 2004 to appreciate the role of village council,* Kebang, *of Rumgong village of the Adis.*
5. Though the crops are grown all the year round, constant engagement is required in paddy cultivation which is the main crops in jhum field. This period has been referred to as main jhum activity, for in other times there are sufficient intervals to organise different social functions.

III

Galo World-view and Resource Use

For material means of existence people of each and every community interact with natural resources individually and collectively. While interacting, faiths, beliefs and practices, in other words the worldview (Redfield, 1953 & 1962; also see Adhikary, 1984) in general, determine the nature, extent and purpose of resource use. In other words, resource use has a supernatural context as reflected on material plane. Particularly in tribal communities it reflects three dimensions of a relationship: human-nature-supernature. Faiths and beliefs speak of the creation myth in general and the relationship between human and nature in particular. Practices on the other hand concern with maintaining and reinforcing this relationship at the time of resource use. The present chapter discusses faiths, beliefs and practices pertaining to land, water and forests which constitute material resource base of the tribal communities like the Galo.

Traditional Galos are ecosystem people (see Gadgil and Guha, 1995:3).They have been depending on ecology not only for their material means of existence but also beyond that. Their beliefs and practices reflect the kind of relationship that exists between human and nature. Nature to them consists of the unknown of which they are often afraid of, which is reflected in their belief of a host of spirits, dwelling in various places, and their impact on human life. It is but natural that between the relationship of human and super-nature there always exists a natural object. For example, in understanding of the concept of *Donyi-Poloism*[1], the philosophical expression of Galo religion, there exist natural objects like *Donyi* and *Polo*. Similarly, appeasement to the supernatural beings that cause diseases is done through the sacrifice of animals/fowls. It is therefore not out of context to state that resources for the Galos are also objects which they use with various terms of reference to the supernature.

The Galo Worldview of Resource and Resource Management

The Galo worldview reflects a bipolar division of resources: the domesticated ones belonging to humankind, and the wild to the ethereal beings. According to Galo folklores, the mythical forefather *Abo Tani*, the first human, had a fight with his elder brother, *Taro* or *Taki* (the spirit brother of *Tani*) over the ownership of resources. It is believed that the fight led to the disruption of peace on earth. Therefore, all the animals and plants requested both of them to divide the resources between themselves and live harmoniously as before.

The division of ownership of resources between humankind and ethereal beings is not exclusive and absolute as far as use is concerned. The ownership of domesticated animals requires the blessings of the deities and ethereal beings for their growth and well being. Similarly, the animals belonging to the *Uyu*(s) are used by human beings by propitiating or through offerings. So this relationship between human-nature and supernature has been used as a frame of analysis of Galo perspective of resources and their management. In other words, the focus is on worldview of the people so that the resource management in cultural perspective is better appreciated. The cultural perspective of the people manifests in different aspects of their life. By focusing on one particular aspect it is not difficult to understand the culture of a people because various aspects of the life are integrated and present the culture-whole[2]. (Pertin, 2009:80). As the topic of research has a focus on resource management, it is but natural to begin with the resource base and management practices in Galo culture.

As has been mentioned, resource and resource management

by people have a trajectory of relationships among human, nature and supernature. This relationship has three dimensions in terms of human-nature relationship, human-human relationship and, of course, human-nature-supernature relationship. Further this relation is not static over time and space. (For details see Redfield, 1953 and 1962; and Adhikary, 1984).

Chart 3.1: Genealogical Chart Showing Origin of Human

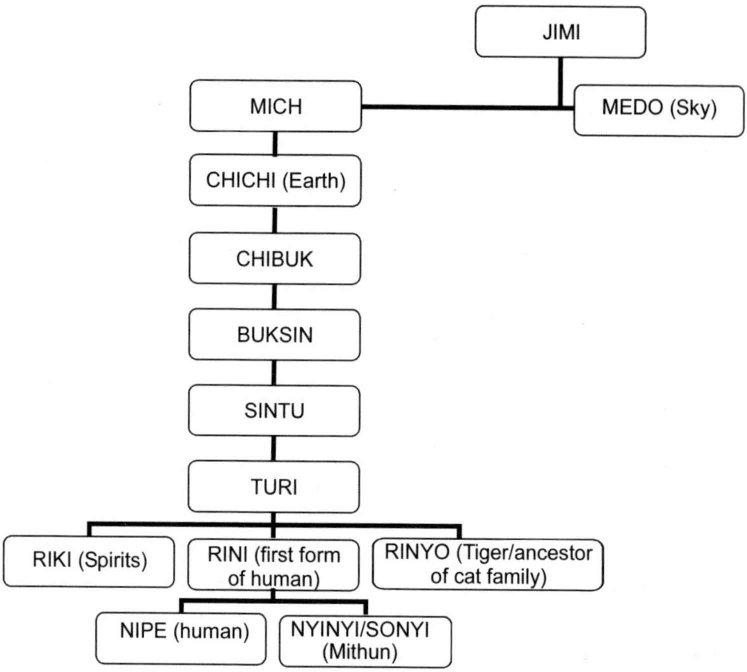

Source: Based on information provided by Mr. Tama Mindo, *a nyibo*

The relationship between human and nature is explicitly reflected in their story or narration of origin of life/human. According to Galo myth, *Jimi Ane,* the creator, created *Medo/ Tale* (the sky) and *Mich.* From *Mich* came *Sichi/Chichi* (the earth). From the union of *Tale* (sky) and *Sichi* (earth) forests with all kinds of trees, bushes and grasses, etc. and animals including *Tani* (ancestor of human beings), *Taki* (ancestor of spirits) and *Tanyo* (ancestor of tiger/cat family) were borne. The Galo address *Sichi* as *ane*, which means *Sichi*, the mother. In this context it is to be mentioned that till *Tani* the Galos trace the genealogy from *Jimi ane* along the female line. From *Tani* the human race came into being. Similarly, from *Taki* the generations of *Uyis* and from *Tanyo* the race of cat families which include *Nyote* (tiger), *Nyopak-Takar* (leopard), *Nyoke* (panther), *Nyoli, Nyomuk* and *Nyoji* (various species of wild cats) came.

All living beings according to Galo mythology share a common ancestor at some point along the genealogical tree. It is evident from the Chart 3.1 that *Turi* is the common ancestor of human beings, animals of cat family, *mithun*, etc. Therefore, human is related to all life forms. As such, their general outlook is that of a "community of being" (see Gadgil, Berkes, and Folke 1993) where human is seen as a part of the nature rather than its possessor[3].

The survival of human itself depends on the survival of the wild. This is reflected in their sayings:

> "*tumsi nyomra lo , hottum lelam go hore lelam go doma rem yobe nyine hage ha rem. tumsi nyomra irga kama, isi opo kama rem mopin e irga kama. sile boso gobo golak go goka kichin gatugo ao go kama rem nyiram re*".[4]

That is, if wild forest is denied of its flora and fauna, the lives of the people will not prosper. In the same manner if the river is denied of fish, then too there will be no life for human beings.

This outlook of the Galo provides ethical imperatives to resource use and management.

Land

According to Galo myth *Tani* and *Taki* were constantly quarrelling over the ownership of land. In order to settle the disputes between them *Donyi Jilo,* the highest priest of the yore, intervened and divided the land into *momen* (land suitable for human use) and *modir* (vertical/land not suitable for human use). *Donyi Jilo* gave *momen* to *Tani* and *modir* to *Taki* with further instruction that their respective descendents would have the rights over their father's land. Despite this division *Taki's* descendent groups namely, the *Doje, Yapom, Pomte-Sarte* and the *Bute-Kamdu*, inhabit trees, streams, caves, rocks and other such landforms within a *momen*. They create problems for the human beings. That is why rituals are performed in their names when human beings use such lands or nearby lands.

The practice of agriculture/horticulture, as the Galos believe, has its origin in the myth where *Abo Tani* by mistake enters into the land of *Mopin,* also called *Digo Lura* (*lura* meaning fence) following *Kipu*, the dog, who chases the deer-*Dumpu*. Both the *Kipu* and *Tani* are captivated. As a plan to escape he kills a rat and puts it under his armpit. After some days a foul smell emits from *Tanis'* body. He accuses *Mopin* for keeping him captive for such a long time and laments over the counted days of his life. Taking pity on his condition *Mopin* releases him and gives him grains which he brings in the ear of the dog. Thereafter, he tries to cultivate which proves to be a futile exercise. So *Mopin* and *Digo Yamo*[5] teach *Abo Tani* the skills and techniques of cultivation. *Digo Yamo* also tell the time of cultivation and informs *Abo Tani* that they would visit him in the form of *Takom Papuk* and *Sii Piyir* (both birds) during that time. Hence, every year just after the beginning of sowing *Mopin* festival is celebrated to seek the blessings of Mopin. When *Ponu*[6] is performed during *Mopin* the lead man/woman narrates the origin of various aspects of culture mainly relating to agricultural practices. For example, *Ojo Toojo Maya* narrates various stages of *jhum* cultivation and another *ponu*, *Go Goi Ya* describes the stages of cotton cultivation along with processing of cotton and weaving of clothes. The *ponu* displays a holistic perspective, for while narrating the stages of agriculture it also makes mention of the time of the year when cultivation should start, various animals and birds which are sighted during various agricultural cycles, and other inter-related topics.

In between the agricultural works various rituals are performed in the field to enhance productivity and to safeguard the crops from pest infestation. Kohli (1997: 81) mentions of the performance of "*Ampu Yolu* ritual for the protection of ...crops from the pest and diseases". Spirits are responsible for the increase in productivity and protection of crops, and so the appeasement of the spirits becomes very important. The priest chants in the glory of *Ampir, Mopin, Pikku* (*Pinku*), *Pirte, Pirlin-Ngurlin,* etc. (ibid).

As per Galo myth, *Yaje Yapom* is the owner of all highlands and forests. And in case a person wishes to cultivate such plots/ lands he needs to propitiate *Yaje Yapom* by performing *Pombek* ritual. Otherwise, misfortune might befall. As per the result of *Pip Roksin*, (omen through egg) a goat/fowl is sacrificed[7].

Though individual ownership over the field and its products is recognized, the rituals are performed collectively and hence the collective solidarity is maintained. *Ampu* ritual is performed for good harvest and protection of the crops from pest, diseases and other natural calamities like excessive rain and heat. It is performed during the flowering time of paddy. The deities, namely *Jeru poru, Pote, Biro-mugli* and *Yapom* are propitiated. Linked to this ritual is the practice of pest management. The day after the ritual, village women go to their respective fields and perform the rite *amsep-misep*. They wrap a mixture of *amtir* (rice powder) and *opo* (fermented rice) into small bundles/ pouches in *oko* (a leaf) which are tied to bamboo sticks; these sticks then are fixed randomly in *jhum* fields. The pest gets attracted to these pouches. The belief is that if such pouches are eaten by the pest or the insect a good harvest is assured.

The ritual, *dir-tachi* is also performed in case of excessive pest infestation. Etymologically *dir* means famine and *tachi* means pest. *Tachi* was responsible for the famine in the past. The ritual is performed in the village. An egg, fowl or a pig is offered in the ritual. Small pouches of all the edible grains and vegetables are made and offered to the *Uyis.* After the performance of the ritual the effigies of the *Uyis,* made of bamboo and various leaves, and the sacrificed animal and fowls along with other offerings are placed in a bamboo raft (*hipe*) and immersed in the river. It is performed to appease *uyis* like *yapom, Nyipo, Doli doga* who are held responsible for causing the infestation. After the ritual, taboo is observed for two days where mobility is restricted. Entry to and exist from the village are strictly restricted.

According Galo myth, famine comes into being after *Abo Tani's* marriage with *Rosi Tami*, daughter of *Dir* (the famine). As *Tani* married *Rosi Tami*, *Diyi Tami*, daughter of *Mopin*, whom *Tani* had married earlier, leaves for *Digo Pine* (the land of *Mopin*). *Diyi Tami* had a magical pot which could prepare enough food for the whole family with only a single grain. Unaware of this, in the absence of *Diyi Tami*, *Rosi Tami* puts two grains which produces a huge quantity of rice. Without any idea of what to do with the excess rice, she asks *Diro-Kibo* (dog of famine) to consume it. When *Diro-Kibo* consumes the excess rice, he also consumes the magical power of the pot. As a result the pot loses its magical power and *Tani* has to face food shortage for the first time. This is the beginning of famine in human society as per Galo belief. Unable to bear the famine *Tani* asks *Diyi Tami* to return to him. *Diyi Tami* agrees on the condition that *Rosi Tami* should leave the house and *Diro-Kibo* should be killed. To fulfil the condition *Tani* drowns *Rosi Tami* in the river and kills *Diro-Kibo.* He throws *Diro-Kibo's* dead body into a water fall. After fulfilling the conditions of *Diyi Tami, Tani* propitiates *Mopin*, who visits *Tani* with gifts of all type of grains and agricultural tools. With Mopin, *Diyi Tami* also comes back to the house of *Tani*. Since then, the Galos believe that *Dir* visits the land of *Tani* every year and with him various pests who destroy the crops. In order to escape famine due to his visit *Galos* perform the *Dir-Tachi* ritual to appease not only to *Dir* but also to various *uyis* who also cause pest infestation.

Forests

There are various studies which have shown the intimate relationship that exists between tribals and their forests (see Roy Burman, 1985; Gadgil and Berkes, 1991 and Gadgil and Chandra, 1992). This relation in case of the Galos is very much evident from their beliefs and practices. It is to be mentioned that nothing in the forest is completely owned by an individual or community. The belief in the control/ownership of the wild by the spirit brother of *Abo Tani* puts a restraint on use of these resources. Traditionally, the use of natural resources was completely regulated by their strong beliefs in soul and various supernatural beings.

The forest is believed to be the abode of spirits. Therefore, for the *Galos*, the various components of forest (animals, trees, water bodies, etc.) are not just physical objects that can be harnessed indiscriminately; but these are living entities which are under the protection and care of certain spirits who may be angered by excessive hunting, fishing or logging by an individual. There is a saying that *maj Motum monna, isi monna nyi rima donna,* which if translated would be "those who hunt and fish a lot do not have a very good life or that they may have premature death". It is believed that the lives (not the soul) of such persons are taken away by the spirits of jungle and water.

The spirits are so feared that even defecating and urinating near big trees, creepers, some rocks or stone and water bodies like river (*hibu*), streams (*higur*), etc. is avoided. Such acts insult the *yapoms* of forest and *yapoms* and *nyipos* (soul of women who die during child birth) living in water bodies. Women, during their period of menstruation, avoid bathing and washing their clothes directly in the water sources. The same restriction is imposed on women after child birth until her bleeding stops.

In the above context the nature is represented in terms of the spirits which are malevolent, always ready to harm human beings. At other times these spirits are perceived as the protector of human and as giver of resources, for example, animals during hunting. Animal killed during hunting are believed to have been given by the *Yapoms*. Whenever it gets dark while a person is in the forest and it is not possible for him/her to return to the village or go to a nearby village, s/he looks for a big tree, rock or a cave to spend the night. The belief is that the *yapoms* dwelling in such places treat them as guest and offer protection from wild animals and other unforeseen accidents. Therefore, when staying in forest is unavoidable, the person first identifies the place where s/he wishes to spend the night and entreats the *yapom* that "I have come to your refuge, so please help me and protect me".

The Galo people normally abstain from felling trees like *hirek* and *hiri* as they are the dwelling places of *yapoms*. But if need arises they fell such trees after performing *pombek* ritual. So rituals are important component in their relationship with nature as it gives some control over the nature by permitting them, for example, felling of trees which normally they are not allowed to. *Kole, Kormi* (variety of wild banana), and *rep-remo*, (a variety of cane) are never cut as they belong to the *yapoms*. Most of the rituals also prescribe taboos on felling of trees, cane, bamboos, etc. as well as hunting and fishing. For example, if the ritual *yapom uyo* is performed, then felling of *kolu* (wild banana), *lunga, konga, tasin, tare, oso* (cane) and *e* (bamboo) are totally prohibited till the following new moon.

No doubt, there is a dualistic relationship between human and nature; at one time it shows antagonism while at the other a strong sense of mutualism.

The *nyote* (tiger), *nyore-takar* (leopard), *nyoke* (panther) and *nyomukh* (another animal of cat family) are only killed when they become threats to human and animal lives. The Galos try to avoid killing these animals as far as possible. According to the Galo folklore, *Tani* (*Rini*) and *Rinyo* (tiger) were brothers. *Rinyo* chose to depart to the forest as he depended on raw meat whereas *Tani* took cooked food; therefore, living together became difficult. Hence, killing of tiger is treated equivalent to committing a murder. When a tiger is killed it is brought near the village and a ritual is performed where the *nyibo* justifies its killing. (Riba, 1998:39-40).

The hunter has to observe taboo strictly. All the villagers are also forbidden from going to field and other villages for a prescribed period. The hunter stays in the *dere*- community hall, for ten to fifteen days, till the performance of the ritual *gapu minam*, whereby soul of the tiger is asked to leave the village. The hunter sleeps in the *bago* of the house for 5-6 months. He observes celibacy for one year. Also ginger and rice paste are tabooed for him for the whole life. Ginger and rice paste are used in festivals and rituals which come under the fold of Galo concept of purity. Since the act of hunter amounts to murder (which comes under pollution) he is to abstain from using the above two things. He is also tabooed from consuming the meat of all the striped animals, birds and even fish till his death.

The performance of rituals associated with hunting discourages indiscriminate killing of animals and birds and encourages maintaining mutual relationship between nature and human. Post hunting rituals are mandatory with the exception of killing of some rodents and birds. In such rituals domesticated animals are sacrificed in exchange of the animal hunted to protect oneself from the wrath of *yapom*. This suggests some form of reciprocal exchange between the *yapom* and human.

Performance of ritual is also related to a myth. It is believed that *Abo Tani* and *Doje* (spirit) stayed together in the same house. Whenever *Tani* hunted a wild bird or animal, *Doje* would complain that it was his domesticated animal or fowl. But *Tani* did not stop hunting wild animals. Out of anger one day *Doje* stole away *Tani's* son *Nyinya* and left the house. *Tani* tricked *Doje* with the help of *Tapen* (bat) and negotiated the return of *Nyinya*. During negotiation *Doje* put a condition that whenever *Tani* would kill wild animals and birds, he should perform rituals with the sacrifice of domesticated animal or fowl in lieu.

Before hunting and trapping, hunters perform *Yabur*[8] (a ritual) by the side of *beda* (road, foot tract). After clearing a small portion of land, the hunter places a few grains of rice and chants hymns to propitiate *Yapom Yaje,* who are owner of the wild animals. The main objective of this ritual is to make hunting and trapping successful. *Kame Panam* (a ritual for hunting, trapping and fishing) is performed on the occasion. Similarly, before felling trees for timbers *Digo Monam* (a ritual) is performed.

There are other rituals relating to hunting and trapping. The important ones have been mentioned as under:

(i) Before a hunting expedition *Motum Pombek* is performed where a fowl is sacrificed and egg is offered to *Chigi Pomchi (Yapom)*, care taker of wild animals and birds. The reason behind this performance is to request *Chigi Pomchi* for providing game animals.

(ii) On successful trapping, especially of animals rather than rodents, *yabur panam* is performed where leaves of *eni* (a bamboo variety) is used to ward off any misfortune that may accompany the trapper.

(iii) After the successful hunting, *Digo Monam*, *Yapom Panam, Kaji Pomji* or *Peka Panam* rituals are performed. There are different rituals for different types animals hunted. For example for, boar, bear, or mountain goat a ritual called *Laklam* is performed with occasional shouts (*ho-e*) on way back to the village. On reaching home another ritual *Piya,* with the offering of an egg or fowl, is performed, to thank the *yapom* for providing the animal. *Digo* ritual is performed for all types of animals hunted.

(iv) After hunting of a bear the ritual *yapom digo* is performed. For animals of cat family such as *Hunyo, Nyore, Nyote,* the ritual *Gaapu* is performed to drive away the spirits of these animals from the village. A *rektum* (pig) is sacrificed to appease the progeny (male) of tiger. Fowl is also sacrificed for *gaapu/erap*.

(v) *Peka*[9] is also performed by hunters. When *Tani* and *Rinyo* (tiger) got separated, the latter put a condition on *Tani* to keep the relationship a secret. In case of disclosure, *Tani* would be killed by *Rinyo*. But during his old age, *Tani* had to disclose the secrecy to his sons under compulsion. So instantly *Tani* was killed. Since *Tani's* sons had no weapon, they requested *Peka* or *Bote-Kate* (god of weapon and bravery) for weapons. *Peka* provided them with weapons which they used to kill *Rinyo* (tiger). In recognition to the timely help, *Tani's* descendants perform the ritual *Kaji-Pomji* to thank him. As Galos have been pursuing hunting activity and using the weapons, which are believed to be the gifts of *Peka*, they perform the thanks giving ritual as a custom.

If rituals are not performed, the *Uyus* like *Yapom Yaje* are believed not to provide animals; rather they are likely to cause harm to the family. The rituals are performed to propitiate or exploit the owners of the big animals and trees. Otherwise, *Doji-Yapom,* dissatisfied deities of the jungle, would torment the man concerned and cause disease and even death. Therefore, rituals are basically performed to propitiate the owners of the jungle and for the escape from unfortunate happenings/sickness of hunter or relatives or to prevent one from being killed by wild animals.

The performance of post-hunting ritual has an element of fear in it, though, the general notion of appeasement is all pervasive. It is evident from the practice of telling lies in the process of appeasement. The hunter does not own up the responsibility of killing the animal; rather he claims *Hima Gejo* (price for carrying the dead) during the appeasement ritual for carrying the carcass which was lying unattended.

Apart from the belief in *yapoms,* seasonal birds like *tako-papok, iti-titi, ciir-piir* etc. which are linked to their agricultural process are not killed.

Adult male members before going to fishing, hunting or trapping are required to maintain distance from female members. The pursuits of hunting, fishing, trapping are also tabooed for the husband of a pregnant woman. Such pursuits are also tabooed for a person for a specific time period after the performance of a ritual. However, there is no movement taboo for the village as a whole in fishing and trapping. But in case of community hunting or killing of big animals by an individual hunter, movement taboo is strictly observed; no one from outside is allowed to enter the village and no one from the village is allowed to go outside the village and even to forest or agricultural fields.

There are also taboos in foraging activities like collection of honey, leaves, roots, fruits etc. *Nginli penam,* large scale collection of honey, is an activity with ritualistic prescriptions. Two days before *nginli penam*, the ritual *Do Pombek* is performed with the sacrifice of two fowls to appease the *Jete-Pomte Do Yapom*[10], the guardian of forest. After performance of the ritual, there is movement restriction for two days. On the third day honey is collected.

The gathering of vegetables and other edible food items from the forest is also regulated in terms of taboos observed after various rituals and rites. For example, after *mopin* and *dirtachi* ritual, movement is restricted and therefore, no activities are undertaken outside. Obviously, during these days works relating to resource use are suspended. After a marriage, in which *Togu*[11] ritual is performed, use of a number of edible forest items is tabooed; some even for a year or so. Plucking or cutting of any sprout is tabooed for both groom and bride for atleast six months[12].

Foraging activity is very important during house construction. The activity and the house itself is a cultural reality. To a Galo, the house itself is not just a physical space but cultural manifestation (see Basar, 2006a:105-118). The origin of house construction is related to their myth about Abo *Tani*, who in the absence of a house had to dwell in caves, on branches of trees and in rock shelters. According to *Lare* and *Pugo*[13] version, it is the spirits *Yirku-Yirte*, *Podi* and *Gute-Gamro* who taught *Tani* the art of house construction and the knowledge of various raw materials to be used. The *Lodu-Karka*[14] group believes that it was one *Nane-Pale*, who with the help of the stem of *ekkam* leaf showed to *Tani* the way each pillar is to be erected during house construction. The folktale narrates the varieties of trees and plants that can be used for construction. Till date they use these trees and plants. Therefore not all the trees or bamboos in the forest are used for construction. There is also a particular period when these can be extracted from the forest[15].

Water

According to Galo myth, at first the sky and earth were together. When they got separated, the sky was levelled, but the earth was not. To level the earth there was a phase of earth quakes and landslides (*Sijak Dojak jakrap*). During this phase the river was buried underground covered by rocks. Life became miserable without water and people tried to make the water flow. This episode is narrated in a poetic form in Galo folklore as presented in Appendix 3.1.

The lore simply means the following: *Agi Bagi* (a spirit in the form of a rat) had knowledge about the water source. He earlier used to drink water from underground. When others came to know about it, all the deities and living creatures requested *Agi Bagi* to bring the water from underground. *Agi Bagi* agreed to do so. He equipped himself with the axe and sword, and started to cut through the ground and worked day and night. After a few days of hard work, he found the water that was hidden below the ground/ rock. But the water refused to flow. It demanded that its flow over the ground should be like a marriage procession and she be decorated as a bride. All the deities accepted the request of the river. So they created fishes and water birds to decorate the river. They also arranged the way for river to flow downward easily.

As mentioned earlier, fishes were created to decorate the river. But the practice of consumption of fishes by the Galo people also has its origin in *Tani*'s time. Along with it is associated the myth of catching fish by the method of poisoning. According to the Galo myth, *Tani* married *Onyor* (wild vegetable, the fruit of which is used as herbal poison). It is said that *Onyor* always fed *Tani* the best of the fishes. One day *Tani* out of curiosity followed his wife and saw that her urinating in the river caused the fishes to die. *Tani* scolded her for doing so and out of shame she ran away into the forest. The Galos believe that the knowledge of catching fish by poisoning came from that time. However, the knowledge was applied much later. This is evident from the *Jaayi Bone* folktale. This tale is narrated in the *ponu Jaayi-e-Bone Jaayie Ja*. In the *Jaayi Bone* tale, *Didu Kubo*, the master of forest and *Bur Tapu*, the master of aquatic animals, fell in love with *Jaayi Bone. Jaayi Bone* married the latter which infuriated *Didu Kubo*. He planned to kill both, but without much success. Finally, *Inbo*, the wild cat, told about *mute-munyo* tree which bears poisonous berries. *Didu Kubo* grounded the poisonous berries and put it into the water. The water became poisonous. *Jaayi Bone* and *Bur Tapu*, unable to tolerate the poison, came out of the water and were killed by *Didu Kubo*.

During fishing activities like *Hito* and *Hile Monam,* the ritual *Sibu Yabur Teknam* is performed to the chanting of a priest to appease the *yapom,* the guardian of the fishing site in the river. A fowl is sacrificed. Thereafter, the priest strikes the river water and the participating members with *eni* leaves as a safeguard against *Yabur*. Three other rituals are also performed in Aalo area. The first one is *Ela gunam*, which is performed only during *hibok* and *hil tumnam.* It is performed to please *yapom- Bus Buro,* the guardian of rivers/water bodies, so that the fish are not driven away from the fishing area. Six fowls are sacrificed for the purpose. Second ritual is *Yeb henam*, performed in all the fishing practices where herbal poison is used. It does not involve any sacrifice or erection of alter; only chanting is done to intensify the effect of poison and cause early death of fish. The third ritual, *Kanyi Kame Panam* is performed in *hibok,* the large scale fishing, where the entire community is involved. In Kabu and Paya villages it is performed when *hibok* is carried out in *Yomgo* river. It is performed after damming the river and just before applying herbal poison. The *nyoga ganam* (chanting) is carried out entire night by the *nyibo* to cause early death of fish. Further, it is also performed to protect human and cattle from diseases. Three fowls are sacrificed in this ritual.

In tribal communities like that of the Galos resource use does not have a material context only. It has a mental aspect and so resource use is rooted in beliefs and faiths of the people. Further the beliefs and faiths have applied dimensions. This is evident in rituals which together with faiths and beliefs influence the ethics of resource use. As a result, in tribal communities in general and among the Galos in particular, the material and mental rootedness in resource perspective puts restraints on resource use.

Appendix 3.1

The Galo Lore of Water Resource

"Agi Bagi Mii Gitum Bume La Rokje Bume La Gekkup Pikup La Gellek Pilek La Lile Litak Em Pirop Kunam E Iss Em Pilen Kube Yu	*Ai Komar E Ako Komar E Rido Komar E Rimen Komar E Ai Ako Billo Dekom Parlo Soto Ku*
Lile Modir Em, Litak Modir Em Ai Budi E, Ako Budi E Ai Ako Budi Dilo Koko Bejim Yo Beku Ju Eku Danam E	*Tangu Jako Be Tadi Jako Be Kamda Jako Be Ramnyo Jako Be Ride Jako Be Ringum Jako Be*
Ribo Jako Be Ridum Jako Be Pipo Jako Be Kada Jako Be Ngirda Jako Be Pero Jako Be Jamen Koko Beju Ka Ela Parlen Toku	*Iss Age Ge Lile Litak Bolo Tangu Tadi Ne Kamda Ramnyo Ne Parlik Toku*
Iss Ara Bolo Lile Narin E Litak Narin E Sinjin Dedo Kuda Eku Danam E	*Pipo Jeli E Kada Jeli E Ride Jeli E Ringum Jeli E Ribo Jeli E*
Ridum Jeli E Ngirda Jeli E Pero Jeli E Jemen Koko Beju Ka Ela Parlik Toku	*Ribo Ne Bangi Be Ridum Ne Jotam Be Ngirda Ne Dumbo Be Pero Ne Ne Temam Be Inge La Into*

NOTES

1. Donyi-Poloism represents the traditional Galo belief system. They believe in sun (Donyi) – moon (Polo) dualism. They perceive the manifestation of their belief system in the two natural objects - the sun and moon.
2. A tribal culture presents holistic perspective and hence a culture is usually studied in its totality of manifestation. Since all components of the culture are inter-related and integrated, the study of one aspect also presents a holistic view. In 2004 a group of 17 anthropology students of Arunachal Institute of Tribal Studies, Rajiv Gandhi University, studied different aspects of life independently in the Padam village of Damro, Upper Siang District, Arunachal Pradesh. Interestingly it was found that the single aspect of the life reflected embeddedness, and thus the inter-related and integrated characteristics of the culture.
3. There are also Galo sayings which prove the human-nature relationship in terms of community of beings. *Jimi Ane Mi Sichi Ane Ne Sine Mone Lok Doi – Esar Lok, Aggu Anchi Lok Bume Jirop Toku. Sichi Bume, Jimi Bume, Hai – Ako Go Nesi – Noje Go, Kine Lokne Go, Ejo – Epo Go, Podo – Pago, Kisi Lokrom Go Bume Jito Ku. Okke Kuda Jimi Bume Sichi Bume, Jimi Api E Bidi Birem Em Tebo Nyobbom, Achi Amen Em, Tapum Taruk Em, Sumne Sene Em, Jubo Galo Em, Tato Tade Em, Jimi Api E Pibuk Nenla, Jimi Api E Sikdum Garo, Michi Mikom, Jimi Api E Pilen To*". That means *Jimi Ane* created all the living things of the world to decorate it. Forests, river, wind, air, water, mountains, fishes, animals, were all created by *Jimi Ane.*
4. Interview with Mr. Tony Koyu on 31st March 2009.
5. *Digo Yamo* is the name of the land of the *Mopin* and it is also the collective name for the people of *Mopin* land.
6. In Galo folk performance lead is given by a woman or man well versed with the *Ponu* songs. Others repeat the lead song while dancing.
7. Before hunting the hunter cleans a portion of the jungle for ritual. The same type of practice is followed by Christian Galos (as reported during field study at Belo village) while clearing jungle for *jhum* cultivation. The difference is that the Christian Galo makes a cross mark on the cleared ground with a stick. They do not perform *pombek* ritual.
8. *Yabur*, literally means misfortune. But it is also the name of the ritual *Yabur* performed to ward off misfortunes.

9. *Peka* is the name of the deity who provided weapons to Tani's sons and is also the name of the ritual performed to appease *Peka.*
10. The Galos believe that a species of bee has its own guardian spirit but when it dwells in a different place it may have a different guardian spirit also. Each guardian spirit has its own name. But *Jete-Pomte Do Yapom* is a common terminology for all guardian spirits of bees.
11. *Togu* is the ritual of the highest order. It has different implications on different occasions. See Riba,2006 for entertainment dimension of *Togu* in a marriage ceremony.
12. For details in marriage related food taboos having implication on resource use see Basar, 2007:206-209.
13. Two major social divisions of the Galo. The Galo community is broadly divided into *Lodu-Karka*, *Lare* and *Pugo*.
14. One of the major social divisions of the Galos. ibid.
15. For example, logs, bamboos and cane for house construction are collected during dark fortnight- the period from full moon to new moon. Materials collected during that period are believed not to be infested by pest and thus have durability.

IV

Indigenous Technical Knowledge in Resource Use: Changing Perspectives

The sustenance of Galo people draws on their knowledge and skill vis-à-vis the use of natural resources. This knowledge and skill when translated into practices form the domain of the people's technology. As the major sustenance activities are associated with land, forests and water the present chapter discusses the technology of the Galos relating to the use of these resources. Indigenous technical knowledge however is a little wider than the technology. It includes both the understanding and the application. The knowledge of classifying, for example, soil types; and their use for different purposes also form into the technical knowledge of the people. The plot the Galo people select and the types of crops they grow depend on their knowledge about the productivity of the land. Similarly, the sowing time depends on the knowledge about the right season.

The discussion on ITK has taken into account activities relating to sources of livelihood and protection of these sources from any damage. For example, agriculture being a source of livelihood has its own technology. But in protecting the crops from pests, birds, animals, the Galo people employ some indigenous technology. Needless to say, ITK is very vast in scope, integrated in nature and institutionalised in the social process when apparently it focuses on livelihood security of traditional people. Within this perspective the ITK has been discussed in relation to resource use.

Indigenous Technical Knowledge in Land Use

The land is used for both cultivation and settlement purposes. The cultivation starts with the selection of the *jhum* plot, which is generally in the month of October-November. Though the *jhum* plots are selected after performing an omen test using egg, it is also guided by the people's knowledge about the land. Usually, on the basis of the duration of fallow period, they classify the *jhum* land into *mobi* and *moro*[1]. (*See* Chart 4.1). Since *jhum* is a cyclic form of cultivation, where there is rotation of the plots, *mobi* has a fallow period of about 10-15 years or less, while *moro* has more than that period[2]. The *moro* lands have well grown forest cover and are considered more fertile and hence more productive. It is to be mentioned that the Galos also use the term *moro* for a virgin forest. Therefore, *moro* land is preferred to *mobi* when there is a choice between the two. They further classify the *mobi* and *moro* into *mohen*, with less moisture and *mobom,* which is sufficiently moist. Therefore, the seeds are broadcast/sown earlier in *mohen;* for example, the *bali* variety of paddy is sown during February-March, while it is March-April in *mobom*. In February-March the soil remains damp and contains sufficient moisture even in *mohen*. That is why, people sow paddy in *mohen* so that the plants grow before the moisture content becomes less and summer heat rises.

Chart 4.1: Classification of Jhum Land

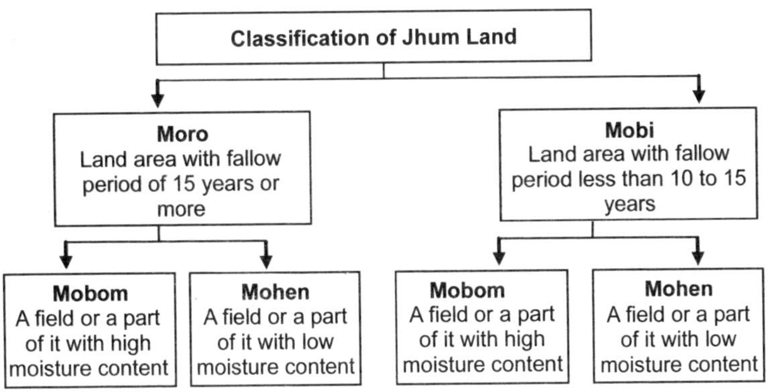

Source: Field study

Generally a *jhum* plot is cultivated for one year only. But sometimes the plot is cultivated for 2, 3, or 4 consecutive years depending on the fertility of the plot[3]. Usually they sow the same crops in all the years. The name of the field cultivated during first year is called *Rikman.* In this field they sow rice, maize, *Meku, Mebo*, *Talar*. When the field is cultivated for the second year is called *Riga*. In addition to the first year's crop they also grow *Enge, Eli, Elak*. During the third year the field is called *Ayo Riga/Abbe/Akak.* The crops of the second year are grown in *ayo riga*.

The Galos determine the fertility of soil by considering its texture. They classify the soil into four types viz, *depo, deli, liye-lire* and *takam*. *Depo* is dark in colour, has more humus and less pebbles. It is considered good for all varieties of paddy and other *jhum* crops and hence is preferred the most. *Deli* is red in colour and has less humus and is not preferred. The yield of paddy and millet in *Deli* is less. *Liye-lire* contains mostly stones and pebbles and are suitable for the cultivation of orange and edible roots like sweet potato, arum, etc. *Takam* consists of clay and is grey in colour. It is good for paddy. Usually a *jhum* plot comprises different types of soil and hence crops are planted according to the texture of the soil. The knowledge about different soil texture results in the mixed cropping pattern which is the characteristics of the *jhum* cultivation.

After selection of the plot, the forest cover is cleared during November-December. First, smaller trees, shrubs, herbs and creepers are cleared. When these dry up, big trees are felled. The felling of big trees is associated with performance of a *pombek* rite. Usually a fowl is sacrificed to appease the *Yapoms*, who are the guardians of the forests and dwell in trees, caves, water sources, etc. While cleaning for jhum cultivation the trees are usually not uprooted as it helps in quick regeneration after the shifting of plot.

The felled trees are chopped into smaller pieces to expedite the drying process. Some of these chopped pieces are carried home for firewood. Fire wood is important for the Galos as they believe that there should be fire in the main hearth especially after sun set. It is therefore, not a surprise to see the continuity of *jhum* cultivation during field study even after the introduction of wet rice cultivation, for *jhum* cultivation still continues to be the source of meeting the requirement of firewood. The logs are also used for preventing soil erosion in the *jhum* field. Piled up logs at slopes are called *paper*. Sometimes logs are also laid horizontally in various parts of the plot to prevent top soil running off. Uprooted weeds are piled up on these logs to dry them so that they do not take root again.

In the months of January and February, the debris is set on fire. To prevent the nearby forest from catching fire, the Galo people clear 1-2 meters of forest around the plot. Even small grasses are removed. Till date there is no record of forest fire arising out of burning of *jhum* plots. It is believed by the Galos that good burning of dried debris enhances the fertility of the soil and also minimizes the growth of weeds.

Traditionally, the Galos have been growing multiple crops like *Tasak* (cotton), *Saa* (tea), *Amo* (rice), *Tami* (millets), *Namdu, Enge, Eli, Elak, Meku, Mebo, Talar, Tape, Tepe, Yaluk, Chukri, Ujuk, Pumpa, Giyi, Bayom, Baka, Peren, Peyak, Nginka, Mali, Take* (ginger), *Kekir* (small variety of ginger) in *jhum* fields. But presently, some of the crops, such as *Tasak, Saa, Pumpa,* are not grown or rarely found in *jhum* fields.

Various cereals and vegetables are grown in the *jhum* plot. The Galos usually cultivate different varieties of paddy[4] namely, *mede, dangum, yamuk, kimin, bali, anker, yabar, dan, patu pama, pumik, lite, kapu, yayo, minre* in different villages depending on soil and climatic conditions. Some of these, like *mede, dangmuk, yamuk, Kapu, yayo,* and *minre* are early varieties of paddy which are grown in the *doso-rike* (that part of *jhum* plot cultivated earlier than the main plot; *Doso-* eaten first, *rike-* cultivation field). Such plots are smaller in size than the main plots. It is cultivated to avoid scarcity of food grains during the lean period i.e., the period between sowing and harvesting in main plots. Maize is also grown along with the early variety of paddy. Seed beds for vegetables like *bayom* (egg plant), *yalluk* (chillies), *kope* (*Solanum sps.*) and *bake* (*Solanum indicum*) are made in the *doso rike* which are later on transplanted to the main plot.

The Galo people follow a time schedule in their agricultural activities based on natural events. For example, when *hir-pir*, (a bird) sings; trees and plants like *kompi* (peach), *jajin, hika, hili, hito-taso* bloom people know that time has come for sacrificing mithun (time for marriage ceremonies) and sowing the *doso yapa* (field for early variety of cereal crops). Similarly, when *hiti-titi* (a bird) sings, *nyan-nyare* (an insect) buzz and trees and plants like *jayo* and *ged-gelli* bloom, the Galo people know that the time has come for sowing in jhum fields. They follow the lunar cycle and hence they use the same term *polo* to refer to the moon and month. They follow their age old indigenous knowledge of knowing time relating to agricultural cycle viz, selection of plot, clearing of forest, sowing of seeds, weeding and harvesting.

Reading of natural events and sighting seasonal animals and birds are common knowledge in every village. Everybody knows it. For example, the people of Basar area say that sowing of seed in main *jhum* plot should start when the *Takkom-papok* bird is sighted. They also believe that sowing and transplantation of all crops should be over before the voice of *hiti-titi* bird is heard. The paddy and maize are sown by dibbling method, using a wooden dibbler; but the millet is broadcast.

Indigenous ways of Pest Control and Management

Since a long past agriculture has been the major source of livelihoods of the Galos. As in modern time, the agriculture was not free from diseases, and damage by pests, animals and birds. So the ingenuity of people has means and ways to avert such dangers.

Pests are great enemies of the farmers. They largely damage plants and crops. But the farmers have the knowledge about and the ways of controlling these pests. Some traditional techniques used by the Galo people in controlling pests are as under:

i) Application of ash especially in the vegetables like brinjal, *lai-sag* (a variety of Chinese cabbage) and other allied varieties in *jhum* plots and *peleks*. Wood ash is said to be effective in controlling insects like apids.

ii) *Tari* (*Rih-rimu/Risu pamu*)/Gandhibugs (*Leptocoryza acuta*) infest the paddy plants at the time of emergence of panicle. It is considered to be one of the major pests. Indigenous method to control *gandhibug* is by fixing wooden or bamboo sticks randomly all over the field. Dead frogs or dried salted fish are tied to such sticks. *Gandhibug* gets attracted to the foul smell emitted by the dead frog and fish. It is then manually killed or the sticks are taken out and burnt.

iii) Another pest called *tali* (Brown Plant Hopper, *Nilaparvata lugens*) causes reddening of the paddy plants and if not controlled in time lead to withering of the plants. The result is very low yield. As a controlling measure, bamboos with leaves are randomly fixed in the fields. The insect gets attracted to the bamboo leaves. They are then manually killed or burnt.

Indigenous Techniques of Scaring off Birds and Animals

The *jhum* fields are usually far away from the settlement area of the village. Therefore, there is a constant fear of the damage of crops by birds and wild animals. The Galos employ various techniques and devices to protect crops from birds and animals. These devices are made from locally available materials.

Birds usually destroy standing crops. The Galos have evolved indigenous methods of driving away birds from destroying the crops. Some of these techniques are as under:

i) *Tajen* is a rope made out of bamboo strips. *Tajen* is tied criss-crossed over the crops to the poles which are erected in various places in the field. Usually *melo,* made of *ipuk* (bamboo scales) or pseudo stems of banana, are hung on the *tajen* at appropriate intervals. Now-a-days pieces of papers, plastics, etc. are used as *melo.* In *tajen* use of plastic and jute ropes have become common these days.

ii) *Bor-bor* is a bamboo pole with 4-5 internodes fixed at different corners of the field. Each of the bamboo poles is split from above, to a measure of one or two internodes, and a *tajen* is tied below the splitting end. The *tajen* is then pulled from the *nakum* (hut in the field) and released. This pulling and releasing produces a sound *'tar-tar'* as the splits strikes against each other. This sound scares the birds away.

iii) *Takop* are small wooden poles erected in different parts of the field. Over this pole a bamboo with its nodes intact at one end, which resembles a cup in shape, is placed upside down. A small hole is made in the bamboo through which the *tajen* is passed and tied to the pole. When the *tajen* is pulled the *takop* produces a sound '*kat-kat'* as the pole strikes the bamboo cup.

iv) *Peta mole* is the scarecrow. It is usually made of torn or old clothes and given different forms. Some resemble birds while others human form.

To prevent wild animals from damaging the crops, they burn unused clothes or chaffs at the periphery of the *jhum* plots. The chaffs burn whole night slowly and last upto the following morning. The smoke and smell emitting from it drives wild animals away.

ITK in Forest Activities

Forest is a major source of material security for the Galo people. It is the ground for hunting and trapping animals which constitute a major source of their food items. Infact hunting supplements to their dietary requirements. Various techniques used in hunting and trapping have been discussed in the following section. In addition to these, forests supply timber and house building materials which they collect in a small scale according to the need. They do not cut all the trees indiscriminately for they have the knowledge of the quality of wood suitable for house construction. The wood, bamboos and cane for house construction are collected during dark fortnight-the period from full moon to new moon. Materials collected during that period are not infested by pest and so last for a long period. Usually the people use simple technology like *dao* and axe and use muscle energy while cutting and transporting.

The Galo people gather edible fruits, roots and leaves from the jungle. While gathering these items they do not uproot the whole plant. They only collect the parts like plucking leaves which promote further growth.

Indigenous Methods of Trapping Animals and Birds

Flesh food is an important source of protein in traditional Galo community. The Galos employ different techniques to get the flesh food. It is to be mentioned that hunting and trapping of animals are the means of obtaining flesh food. Apart from use of bows and arrows, and gun, Galos also use traps to catch wild birds and animals. Different types of traps are used for various animals. The traps are made of locally available materials. The trapper first identifies the tracks, *bepa,* usually used by the animals, through footprints. The traps are usually fixed on the *bepa.*

Some of the frequently used traps by the Galos to catch animals and birds are as under:

1. *Gore*: It is a bow shaped trap used for catching birds and small rodents. A small hole is dug where the bait is kept and the trap is fixed over it.
2. *Gumdi:* It is the cage trapping methods. The case is made of bamboo and has two rooms. In one of the room the bait, like fowl or animal is kept. The wild animals like tiger, wild dog, leopard etc. get attracted by the sound of the decoy and enters into the trap. Upon entering the wild animal releases the trigger and the door shuts, trapping the animal.
3. *Hitik:* This is a form of snare trap and usually used for trapping birds. The rope used to make the noose is fixed in bamboo or wood. Tension is induced by pulling the

rope and supported by a trigger which is fixed near the noose. Sticks about 3-4 m are erected horizontally in both sides of the trap to prevent the birds from taking side path. When a bird enters into the trap, the trigger gives away and the bamboo is pulled up which tightens the noose around the leg or neck of the birds.

4. *Hogum:* In *hogum* heavy plantain or tree trunks or bamboo platform with weights like heavy stones are used. These are raised high on a tree with the help of a rope attached to a trigger fixed on the ground. It is specially used to catch big animals like bear or porcupine. As the animal steps on the trigger the rope is released and the weight falls upon the animal. *Hogum* may or may not involve the use of bait.
5. *Koma*: It is a trap made of bamboo or wood. Spikes made of bamboo or wood are fixed on bamboo or wood which is kept in tension by bending it with the help of a trigger. The trigger is attached to a rope which is tied to the trunk of a nearby tree. When the animal steps on or touches the rope it lets go the trigger and the bent bamboo in tension gets released. The spikes hit the animal. This results in the death of animal. *Koma* is made with the help of a bow and arrow. It is especially used to hunt animals like tigers, leopards and other large mammals.
6. *Odo:* It is a type of deadfall trap. It is used to catch rodents and birds. It consists of a large, heavy object, such as a rock, which is propped up by a stick, rod or other trigger mechanism. Often, bait is placed under the heavy object. When an animal or bird goes in for the bait, it will usually bump into the trigger mechanism, causing the heavy object to fall and crush it.
7. *Poto*: It is a snare trap where the animal is caught by its neck. A small wooden post is erected. The trigger, a U-shaped clip is fastened to the upper end of the post. A rope attached to one end of the U-clip is fastened to a tree and pulled to induce tension. The rope runs

through the whole length of the U-forming a noose at the other end. If an animal pass through the noose, the former end of the U-clip releases the rope and the noose fastens usually in the neck of the animal as the branch of the tree pulls up.

8. *Pochik*: It is similar to *poto* but simpler than the former. *Pochik* is the simple snare. One end of the rope is fastened to a wooden stump while the other end forms the noose. The noose is held with small twigs. When an animal passes through the *pochik* the noose fastens around the neck of the animal.
9. *Teru Runam*: This is the pitfall method. A pit is dug and then covered with twigs, dried leaves, etc. When an animal passes through such covering it falls into the pit and gets caught.
10. *Uju*: It is a snare trap used for catching rodents. The process starts with the making of a track for the rodents by laying a piece of wood across the stream. The wood is left undisturbed for two weeks to a month or more. When the hunter feels that the track is being used regularly by the rodents then he fixes a trap. A long bamboo or wood is fixed at one end of the piece of wood and pulled to provide tension with the rope attached to its upper end. The trigger is triangular in shape and is made of bamboo with noose. When rodents enter into the noose the tension is released and they are trapped.

Indigenous Techniques of Fishing

The Galo people employ different techniques in fishing. There are various techniques used in different months or seasons of the year. There are also techniques which are used through out the year. Most of the fishing takes place during winter season.

The Galos organise individual, small group or community fishing for various reasons, from supplementing the diet to ritualistic purpose. Depending on the micro habitat of fishes in different rivers the people have evolved various techniques of fishing. More over, the techniques also vary across the gender. Some important techniques of fishing are as under:

1. *Lipum*: It is a stone structure made for catching fishes in rivers. The structure is either a pile of stones and boulders, round in shape or a small circular stone enclosure. The structures are made from October to mid-December in different parts of the river where water is shallow and current is normal. Fishes take shelters in the cavities of the structure. The people start caching fishes from mid December from the cavities using *Hisir/Chirgo* (bamboo -made enclosure) and *Hidir* (an oval shaped bamboo basket trap).
2. *Jile/Hile Monam*: This refers to fishing practice in deep water in a river which usually takes place in September and October months. In Tirbin area if this fishing method is carried out during the summer months it is called *jile monan,* while if it is in winter it is called *Ngocha jile.* People use suitable fishing instruments and techniques and continue fishing for a week or more at intervals depending on the availability of the fishes. In a suitable part of the water they make *ngomam* by piling up wood, leaves and stones. The upper end and lower end of the deep water is closed with *chire* (a porous bamboo mat) to prevent fish form escaping. From the lower end the fishes are driven towards the upper end. The upcoming fishes are frightened by beating the water. Finally the fishes take shelter in the *ngomam.* The *ngomam* is then enclosed with *chirbak* (finely twilled bamboo mat) and *tam,* herbal poison, is applied. Fishes are then collected using different methods.
3. *Bokjek Tumnam*: This is group or community fishing which is done from May to July. Bund is made usually in the subsidiary channels of the river with bamboo mats (*echir*). Bunds are constructed at two portions; one at the upper end of the subsidiary river, where it branches off from the main river; and another at an appropriate place at the lower end. The bund at lower

end is first constructed and *takom,* the fishing trap, is fixed. Sometimes food items like left over rice, *apong* (rice beer) residues are used to lure the fish. A person called *makki rora ne,* is entrusted with the job of observing the movement of the fish. When it is felt that the fishes could be collected, the point, from where the subsidiary river branches off from the main river, is closed with *echir. Tam* is not used. This method is used twice or thrice to catch fishes.

4. *Jigo Tonam/Habsum henam*: It is fishing with scoop-net. Four long sticks are tied to four ends of the net. It is usually practiced in streams or small rivers. The water is channelised to pass through a specified place (*happa*) by blocking the water with porous bamboo mat. Few flat stones in rectangular shape, called *ngoi dumpa* are placed in the *happa.* A platform, where the fisherman sits, is constructed over the *happa* with bamboo. The net is inserted into the water with the help of four sticks. When the fisherman observers that fish are passing through the net, the net is pulled up to catch the fish. Species like *orpu, ngopi* etc. are caught.
5. *Jipe/Hito/Hipe/Sipe Panam*: This method involves making of a bund in the river with a single outlet (as in villages of Tirbin, Basar and Gensi) or sometimes with two outlets (as in Kabu and Paya village). Large bamboo baskets called *jire dumpa,* are fixed in such outlets to catch the fishes. This technique is followed from August to October. This is a group activity. *Jipe* method involves contribution of labour from all the male members of the village. It takes two-three days for collection of materials and another four-five days for the construction of *jipe.* It is mainly practiced during the month of August.
6. *Takom Ganam*: Takom is a tubular trap made of bamboo. A number of traps are fixed in various points in a river or stream to catch fishes. This technique is mostly used during *ngoru chanam,* the time when fishes come upstream to lay eggs. The time varies between

October and November depending on the temperature of the place. In Ringi village October is the month for *ngoru chanam* while in others it is November. However, this technique is used from October to March in individual fishing as the river streams become narrow and the water shallow.

7. *Rime Menam/Rigo Gonam*: This is a group activity of female members. Here the fishing equipment i.e. *raju*(s), used by women are fixed in a line across a river or stream. The participation of women folk then drive the fishes from downstream towards the *raju* by walking in groups in the river. It is done in March to May.
8. *Ga -ak/Eker Rinam*: This is a technique in which a number of hooks with baits, suspended from a rope or wood or bamboo are laid across a stream or river usually from April to October.
9. *Potuk Tuknam*: This is a technique used by female folks from June to August to catch fishes in muddy water of flooding streams by thrusting and lifting *raju,* the fishing implement.
10. *Tase/Tach Karnam*: From November to March crabs are found nestling below the stones lying in the river bed/ streams. The practice of collecting crabs by lifting or removing these stones is called *Tase/Tach Karnam.*
11. *Taju Karnam*: It is a group activity where tadpoles and fingerlings are collected with bare hands. It is carried out in March till May.
12. *Jibok/Hibok Penam*: The technique is same as that of the *bokjek tumnam* except that *hibok* is a day activity. This technique of fishing can be used all the year round in the stream if found suitable, but it is appropriate only in summer season in a river.
13. *Tajum/Tasum Kunam*: This is usually a female activity in which *tasum* (shrimps) are caught using *raju*. Tasum Kunam is carried out through out the year, but it is suitable from November to April.
14. *Rib Dinam*: In this technique, used through out the year, the stalk of *ekkam* leaf is used to fix a bait, usually *eku*

tachi (the insect found inside tender bamboos), earthworm, small grasshoppers, etc. This technique is used to fish *ribo* and *tayek.* When this technique is used for catching crabs usually baits are not used.

15. *Ngoro Ronam*: It is done round the year. Bow and arrow, with a line, is used to catch fish.
16. *Ga-Ak/Eker Ernam*: Angling, *Ga-Ak/Eker Ernam*, is also done anytime around the year. Usually *eni* variety of bamboo is used as the rod. In early times fibre of *tamak* tree was used as line, but now-a-days nylon ropes are used instead. The *gekar*, (hook) is made of iron.
17. *Ngoi Apnam*: *Ngoi Apnam* (bowfishing) is carried out through out the year in shallow water.
18. *Ejap/Esap Ernam*: It is a fishing practice carried out with the help of cast net and is practised all the year round.
19. *Musri Ranam:* Mosquito nets are used for fishing and the practice is usually carried out during the night time. This is a recent technique adopted by the Galos.
20. *Ergo Tongnam:* This is a technique of fishing by using bamboo rafts which involves a group of two or more persons. In each raft there are two persons; one rows the raft and the other fishes. In a long bamboo, usually of *eni* variety, several nooses are made with *tamak* rope (now nylon rope is used). The bamboo is thrust in the river and pulled out and the fish are caught in the noose which tightens around their body or the gill. In case of group fishing, four-five rafts are positioned upstream while two rafts from downstream scare the fish, making much noise by beating the river with their rowing bamboo poles and drive the fish towards the rafts. It is usually practised during winter months from October to February.
21. *Heyak Henam:* It is also a type of angling practised in deep water to catch large size fish like *tingir.* Two hooks are tied together back to back. The line is very long and hence is required to pass through 3 or 4 nooses attached to the rod. Bait is not used in this type of fishing. The fish gets hooked in the body or gill and struggles to escape. The angler does not pull out the fish directly but lets the line

loose whenever necessary till the fish gets exhausted. Then the angler pulls the fish out.

22. *Tapi Monam:* This is a technique of fishing using *tapi* (leaves of a reed growing in the river bed), *tare* (a cane variety with big thorns) and light. Near the bank of a river *tapi* and *tare* are kept spreading as fish move towards the bank in the night. The leaves of the *tapi* look bright in dark night. So fish move away from the spread in different directions. But people waiting downstream with the *miir*, a glowing torch, drive them towards the spread. On seeing the glowing light and noise made by the people while driving, fish suddenly push back towards the spread of *tapi* and *tare* where some of them get caught in the thorns of *tare*.
23. *Taju Rula:* This is a practice of catching frogs in banks of streams or rivers, especially in the month of October. The people search for the frogs in night using *tatik miir*, a bamboo lit torch and catch them with hands.

The Galo people have spread over a wide range of micro-habitats. The faith and belief relating to resource use is guided by their general worldview but the practices are influenced by specific environmental condition. The fishing technique of one village may not exist in other villages, but the technique is not an isolated phenomenon of the Galo culture. For example *ergo tongnam* and *tapi monam* are known to be practised in the river *Yomgo*. This practice does not exist in the rivers of other sample villages. But people in other villages do not feel the practice as an alienated one when they learn that this is a practice followed in a Galo village. Similarly, the practices in the performance of rituals, in economic pursuits, etc. vary from one micro-habitat to the other. In many sample villages *riga,* reciprocal community appropriation of labour, still exists in WRC practice.

Changing Perspectives

The traditional life of the Galo people has been exposed to state induced development interventions. As a result changes have taken place in many aspects of their lives. These changes are in the nature of modification, replacement or addition. In the field of agriculture TRC and WRC are getting importance. As a result there is change in technology in terms of agricultural inputs. In the new methods plough bullocks, power tillers and tractors are used. Infact ploughing technique is completely new as it did not exist in shifting cultivation.

The practice of keeping *jhum* fields fallow is a technology of recuperating the soil fertility. Moreover, a field is cultivated at best for three years with a mixed cropping pattern for subsistence requirement. Shifting cultivation does not require provision for permanent irrigation. Contrary to the practices in *jhum* cultivation chemical fertilisers are applied to maintain the fertility of the soil. High yielding varieties of seeds are used. In WRC and TRC people use pesticides in place of earlier techniques used in *jhum* fields. Mono cropping is practised in WRC and TRC fields and the fields are cultivated every year without any fellow period. Moreover, the cultivation is seasonal in nature unlike the *jhum* cultivation where mixed and multiple crops are raised. There is a decline in shifting cultivation. Further during field study it was noticed that high yielding variety of paddy seeds are used in *jhum* fields in many villages. As a result the traditional varieties are gradually disappearing. In villages nearer to urban centres these traditional varieties have almost disappeared.

Traditionally, foraging was the major source of obtaining fruits and fish from the nature. That is why horticulture was not a practice in Galo community. But in recent years horticulture has been a major source of livelihood. In almost all the villages there are orange, pineapple and pear trees. In some there are gardens also. Because of the growth of horticulture in Galo area a fruit processing unit was establish at Nigmoi during early part of 1980s.

Rivers are the major source of obtaining fish. People use to catch fish individually or in groups. But consequent upon government's intervention there are people's fish pond in study villages of East Siang district. Even in few villages in West Siang district people's fish ponds were noticed. The traditional fishing techniques are not widely in practice in many villages. The rivers are leased out to fisherman from outside who use drag nets to catch fishes. Infact, river tracts are now privately owned. Nevertheless, the owners of the rivers do not restrict the villagers from fishing for consumption purpose. Earlier in community fishing or in group fishing herbal poison was used. In recent years the chemical poison and blastings are used to catch fish in a large scale for commercial purpose. Even river beds have found a new use. In many villages nearer to urban centres quarrying has emerged as a new avenue of employment.

Forest resources are traditionally used for subsistence needs. Timbers, canes, thatch, bamboo, etc. were extracted for construction of houses in the village. But in recent years these forest resources are found to be used for commercial purpose. From the very beginning of the development initiatives in the State timbers were supplied to railways. In addition, canes and bamboos are sold within the state and outside for making of furniture. In various urban centres in study area a number of furniture shops were observed. Timbers were also found supplied to these furniture shops. The demand for timber resulted from the demand for benches, desks, almirahs, cots, tables, chairs in government offices and business concerns. The neo-elites also use these furniture pieces. The commercialisation of forest resources has a favourable place in various forest policies. The forest policies like Indian Forest Act, 1927, Forest Policy of 1952, Forest Conservation Act, 1980, have commercial dimension[5]. Arunachal Pradesh Anchal Forest Reserve (Constitution and Maintenance) Act 1975 (which came into force from 12th January 1976), amended in 1981 and further in 1984 as Arunachal Pradesh Anchal and Village Forest Reserve (Constitution and Maintenance) Amendment Act, 1984 also promotes commercialisation of forest resources. The forest resources have found a market beyond the village community at district, state and national level.

The Galo people gathered vegetables, roots, shoots etc. for their own consumption. But it was found that these items have got a demand in urban centres. People from remote villages bring such items and sell them in the market at major urban centres[6] of Galo dominated area. Obviously, the foraging items for self consumption have a commercial dimension in recent years.

NOTES

1. The Galos also classify *jhum* land on the basis of the duration of exposure to sunlight. *Jhum* fields with longer duration of sunlight are called *moba,* and with shorter duration *moyum.* In fact land which does not receive any sunlight is also called *moyum.* Normally, for *jhum* cultivation *moyum* is not preferred to.
2. The data on fallow period is based on field study in villages with more population and having exposure to development forces. In interior villages which usually have less population the fallow period is about 20-25 years.
3. A single plot is also cultivated for more than one year when a family due to taboos or other reasons cannot clear a new plot in time.
4. There is a phonetic variation in the names of the paddy varieties in different Galo areas. For example *bali* in Basar, Tirbin and Aalo area is pronounced as *yali* in Siru Tali and Belo (Yinyo) villages.
5. A provision in the Forest Policy of 1952 is explit with regard to the commercialisation of forest resources. In Arunachal Pradesh Anchal and Village Forests Reserve (Constitution and Maintenance) Amendment Act, 1984, Clause (b) of Article 6 (2) reads, "for the preservation, reproduction, and disposal of trees and timber and other forest produce in the Anchal Reserve Forest". Obviously, 'disposal' has a commercial connotation. The commercialisation aspect was so destructive that the Arunachal Pradesh Forests (Removal of Timber) Regulation Act 1983 clearly focused on administrative control and regulation on removal of timber outside Arunachal Pradesh.
6. Due to occupational change many Galo people have migrated to urban centers. In these centers food items like shoots, leaves and roots are not available. But their food habit has not changed much. They still consume many traditional food items. So people in remote villages collect these items easily and send them to urban centers for sale. This is facilitated by improved transport. Therefore, it is not a surprise to find leafy vegetables, roots and bamboo shoots from Galo area in Itanagar market.

V
Findings and Analysis

The changes in the resource use are the outcome of state induced development interventions. There are policies and programmes in this regard which have influenced the purpose and extent of resource use. In the emerging situation resources are being used in new ways, for two distinct purposes. Firstly, the Galo people use the resources in the traditional way. Secondly, the resource use has also a commercial purpose. Diversified individual interests in resource use have emerged in a significant way. This chapter briefly discusses government initiatives which have brought about changes in resource use in Galo area. Focus is on earlier period of development to understand the dynamics to which people were exposed in the beginning. It is found that the Galo people have responded well to the new ways of utilising resources initiated by government programmes. The discussion on new ways of resource use also highlights traditional values in relation to the emerging situation.

Land Resource

There is a change in agricultural practices and thus in the use of land resources. In plains and valleys in West Siang and East Siang districts people practise wet rice cultivation. In hills of Upper Subansiri and West Siang district terrace cultivation exists along with the traditional practice of shifting cultivation. In addition to this horticulture and fisheries activities have emerged giving a new dimension to land use. The emerging cultivation practices are the result of introduction of crop varieties, HYV seeds, irrigation facilities and schemes for land reclamation and fisheries development.

Land Development

Land reclamation for permanent cultivation in the state in general and in Galo areas in particular has been on priority since independence and still continues unabated in different land use practices other than agriculture. Time series data are not available, but for some years, data on land reclamation are recorded for Galo areas of the then Abor Hills district and present West Siang district. In 1951-52 under normal development fund and under Assam Governor's Earth Quake Relief Fund about 179 and 131 acres were brought under WRC respectively at an expenditure of ₹ 1488[1]. For example, in 1972-73,464 ha of land were developed for cultivation under normal agriculture scheme, CD Block, and crash programmes combinedly in West Siang which was known as Along Sub-division of Siang District then. (GoAP (a), 1972-73:51). In 1996-97, 1997-98, and 1998-99 a total of 16 ha, 20 ha and 37.5 ha have been reclaimed for agricultural activities. (GoAP (a), 1997-98, 1998-99 and 2000-01).

In study villages initially it was reported that government had initiated the steps for land reclamation but the villagers in general converted suitable land in the river beds for WRC by themselves in due course. The government initiatives were sometimes subsidised while at others ended up with persuasions only. Terrace fields were observed in Belo, Beyar, Ronya, Hyder and Digbak villages of Upper Subansiri and in Yiga, Ratak Gamlin and Chekor Lombi villages of West Siang. These fields were developed by the people themselves. In Paya there are two cases of developing WRC fields into fish ponds, one of which was again reclaimed as a WRC field. Preparation for WRC was a self initiative while its development for fish pond was government subsidised. Further, re-conversion to WRC was also done through self initiative. In Lite Boje it was reported that in early part of 1970s the government used to pay ₹ 150 to ₹ 300 as incentives to develop one *pura*[2] of land for WRC. In some villages (names are withheld) people have received government subsidy to develop land for cultivation of citronella, cardamom, orange, ginger and other horticultural crops as per government records. But in those villages land has not been developed for above crops as in many cases the crops did not exist. In some villages when the researcher interacted with the beneficiaries from the list collected from the concerned departments, it was found that they have never received subsidies for the purpose mentioned. PRA sessions reveal that Panchayat members and other village elites in connivance with the government officers have received the subsidy money against the name of the beneficiaries from concerned villages.

Crop Diversity

Traditionally people followed diverse cropping pattern in their *jhum* fields (ICAR, 1983:18-19; Sachchidananda, 1989:57; Sharma, 2003:22). Usually they cultivated paddy, maize, millet, barley, job's tear, tapioca which were also included in the self sufficiency strategy of food production. Along with some of these crops, a number of new crops suitable for both dry land and wet land cultivation were also introduced. Among the new cereal crops mention may be made of wheat which was not in the basket of traditional crops of the people. Vegetables like potatoes, horticultural crops like apple, pineapple, etc., and commercial crops like mustard, ginger, tobacco, sugar cane, turmeric, chillies, cotton, etc. were introduced. (GoAP, n.d.:14). Even for traditional varieties of crops superior varieties of paddy, maize, millet, barley, etc. were distributed free in the border areas and at subsidised rates in the rest of the agency[3]. In course of time quite a good number of horticultural crops including orange, pears, litchi, grapes, kiwi were introduced. The production of fruits and spices during 2004-05 has been recorded at 140605 MT[4]. Similarly, commercial crops also include a wide range of vegetables and other crops including cardamom, pepper, musk *dana*, various types of oil seeds, etc.

HYV Seeds

Increased production is one of the factors of food self sufficiency. HYV seeds contribute to increased production in the improved agricultural methods. The Government supplied HYV seeds not only for WRC and TRC but also for improving productivity in shifting methods of cultivation. It is to be noted that superior varieties of paddy, maize, millet, wheat, barley and mustard seeds worth ₹ 1.27 lakhs were distributed free in the border areas and at subsidised rates in the rest of the areas in the Agency (GoI (NEFA), 1965-66:6).

In 1960s also improved seeds were distributed. [See various Annual Administration Reports of GoI (NEFA)]. It is to be mentioned that in 1962-63 under CD Programme 1104 maunds of improved seeds were distributed. GoI (NEFA), 1962-63:12).

The emerging crop variety in West Siang district has been the result of initiatives from both government and people. In Jomlo, near Aalo, a seed farm was established as early as 26th December 1968[5]. The department of agriculture has introduced various new crops, both improved and high yielding varieties of the existing crops to augment productivity. Before 1968, Taichung native variety of paddy was introduced in villages nearby Along[6]. Way back in 1969, IR-8 was reported to have been introduced in Kamba and Basar areas[7]. Through demonstration farms[8] and organising participation of farmers in agricultural exhibitions[9], the government also encourages cultivation of non-traditional crops. It is reported that in 1972-73, 400 ha were brought under improved seeds and 484 ha under high yielding varieties of seeds. (GoAP (a), 1972-73: 53).

Though government initiative continues, people purchase improved and high yielding varieties available in the market. As many crops like ginger, mustard, vegetables have been commercialised farmers use both the government and market sources for obtaining seeds. It was reported during field study that a few individuals have introduced non-traditional crops in a very small scale which they learnt from neighbouring areas.

The extent of crop variety depends on the nature of

exposure. Villages nearer to market have more varieties, both traditional and non-traditional, than villages in remote areas which produce traditional varieties sometimes for the market also. Further, the villages practising both jhum and WRC have more varieties of paddy than those practising either of the two. In villages like Siru and Belo, the numbers of non-traditional crops are very few, whereas it is quite high in villages like Darka, Kabu and Paya[10]. In these villages the jhum practice has not been totally disappeared and therefore traditional crops still exist, though declining. But in case of non-traditional crops these villages are ahead of other sample villages due to demand in nearby Aalo market. The crop diversity in a village depends on the types of land use such as *jhum*, WRC/TRC, horticulture, plantation, vegetable, etc.

Irrigation

In Agricultural Census 1985-86, 65.93 percentages of total holdings in West Siang were recorded irrigated either wholly or partly. The percentage of net irrigated area to net area sown was recorded at 30.32. Further, under different crops like rice, maize, millet, sugarcane, vegetables, and wheat only 6651 ha of rice field were irrigated. (Dutta Choudhury, 1994: 140-141). By March 2007 total area irrigated in the district has increased to 13,345.2 ha out of which 10, 119 ha are in Galo inhabited circles.

In West Siang, people of some villages were aware of the importance of irrigation for permanent cultivation before independence, though, the construction of irrigation channels is on priority in post-independence agenda. In Kabu, while Mr. P.L.S. James, Assistant Political Officer, persuaded for permanent WRC, people had constructed irrigation channels[11]. Just after the earth quake in 1950, people in Tadin villages started permanent cultivation and dug irrigation channels[12]. Siru Irrigation Channel, with self initiative of the people of Kamki village, was constructed in 1979 to irrigate 585 acres of already developed WRC and TRC[13]. No doubt the Panchayat leaders emphasised on priority of irrigation in the Zilla

Parishad meeting at Aalo in 1978[14]. From governments initiatives irrigation projects were constructed in many villages under different programmes. Mention may be made of the Kombo M.I.P under 20 point economic programme and inauguration of Gensi M.I.P. on 6th September 1978[15].

In study villages irrigation facilities are available where people practise TRC and WRC. For irrigation in terrace fields nearest streams are directly channelled into the plots. But in case of WRC, the field and streams are connected with canals. The irrigation channels are constructed by the people sometimes on self help basis and sometimes on subsidy for the manual labour. The technical aid and cost of construction of sluice-gates were borne by the administration or concerned department. In Lite Boje when the Minor Irrigation project was not successful the people themselves have dug channels to irrigate their fields[16]. The government also promotes alternative sources wherever feasible. AoP [GoAP (a), 2002-03] records 3 beneficiaries under digging of well scheme in West Siang district.

Supply of Tools and Implements

The standard and type of agricultural tools and implements follow the technique of cultivation. Under age-old practice of shifting cultivation minimum agricultural tools are used and land is not ploughed. (GoAP, n.d.:33). Therefore, in traditional system of agriculture, people use simple tools, many of which, like *dao,* have multipurpose uses. These tools and implements consisting of dibbling sticks, scrapper, *dao* and axe are not suitable for WRC and TRC fields. That is why from the very beginning the Department of Agriculture, Arunachal Pradesh has been supplying improved tools and implements appropriate for the improved agricultural methods. Tools and implements suitable for the purpose of agriculture were supplied free of cost in border areas and at subsidised rates at other places of the state.

Records are available from 1950-51 on the supply of implements for the purpose of modernising agriculture[17]. In 1951-

52, 57 pick axes, 120 shovels, 400 Abor daos, 139 hoes and 151 felling axes were supplied to the farmers in the then Abor Hills districts in which present West Siang district was a constitutent part[18]. In 1962-63 agricultural tools and implements cost ₹ 0.38 lakhs, which in 1963-64 rose to 2.01 lakhs. (GoI (NEFA), 1962-63:7; 1963-64:6). These tools and implements were distributed both under normal and CD programmes. In 1962-63 1162 numbers of improved agricultural implements were distributed under CD schemes. (ibid., 1962-63:12). The tools and implements normally included Tata hoes, garden rakes, pick axes, felling axes, crowbars, shovels, threshers etc. which cost 1.25 lakhs in 1965-66. (ibid., 1965-66:6).

AoPs of 18 years from 1983-84 to 2005-06 record 26,923 hand tools supplied to the farmers of West Siang district. In AoPs of 1983-84 and 1984-85 the number of tools supplied was 6032 and 6500 respectively. In 1990s the number declined to less than 2000. The AoP 1997-98 records only 732 hand tools. From 2000-2001 it has further declined; and the AoPs of 2004-05 and 2005-06 record 112 and 12 number of hand tools respectively.

The most important aspect of transformation of hill agriculture is the shift in the use of muscle energy to animal and mechanical energy. Mention may be made of 67 pairs of work animals supplied to the farmers in the year 1963-64 and 73 pairs of bullocks supplied to progressive cultivators in 1964-65 on 50 per cent subsidy basis. (GoI (NEFA), 1963-63:5; 1964-65:10). Similarly, in 1965-66 and 66-67, 36 and 60 pairs of bullocks were distributed respectively. (ibid. 1965-66:6; '66-67:6). In 1966-67 also another 70 pairs of bullocks were supplied under CD schemes. (ibid. 1966-67:21). In recent years supply of working animals have been replaced by the supply of machineries in many districts. In West Siang district the supply of work animals was an important strategy of transformation of hill agriculture. AoPs of 1983-84, 1984-85, 1986-87, 1988-89 and 1993-94 record 100 pairs of work animals distributed in the district to the farmers on subsidy.

Mechanisation of agriculture began with demonstration of the use of the power tillers, tractors, etc. in Government agricultural farms. The main objective of introducing improved tools and implements was to add efficiency to the muscle power. Then these machineries were supplied to the farmers on subsidy. AoPs of 1992-93 and 1994-95 record 30 and 85 machineries like paddy de-husker, pump set, oil expeller, sugarcane crusher, flour mill, etc. which were supplied for mechanisation of agricultural sector in West Siang district. The scheme of supplying agricultural tools and implements free of cost or at subsidised rates continues. AoPs from 1999-2000 to 2008-09 record 47 tractors except during the year 2005-06 and AoP of 2006-07 records 20 power tillers supplied to the farmers in the district for mechanisation of agriculture.

Fertilizer

In the present West Siang District (formerly Along sub-division of Siang Frontier Division) no record is available of the area brought under fertilizers. So is the case in Upper Subansiri and East Siang districts for Galo villages. However, in West Siang district 540 ha were recorded under plant protection measures in 1972-73. (GoAP, 1972-73:52). In 2007-08, 800 ha were reported having been covered under fertilizers and plant protection measures each in the district. But in study villages the supply of fertilizers shows an erratic trend; and not all the villages availed of fertilizer scheme. For example, in Piri 5 beneficiaries, in Kabu 4 and in Darka 3 were recorded having availed of fertilizer scheme only in 2002-03. For these and other study villages no record is available for subsequent years in the concerned department of beneficiaries availing fertilizer scheme. However, during field study in Tapo, a farmer was found spraying pesticide in his farm which as he reported was obtained from VLW. In villages like Belo, Kabu, Siru-Tali, farmers largely use DDT to protect their crops. Some farmers in Darka, Kabu and Tapo villages were reported using weedicide[19] indiscriminately which they purchase from the market as the supply from the concerned department is not found adequate.

Horticulture

In Arunachal Pradesh, people in general were not interested in horticultural crops till 1962-63, though government had established many farms for the purpose. But in West Siang district interestingly there were mango and guava trees in Garu village by 1957[20]. Topographically, West Siang district falls under mild tropical, sub tropical and semi temperate agro climatic zones and therefore, is suitable for the cultivation of litchi, banana, guava, papaya, jackfruit, coconut, black pepper, ginger, turmeric, vegetable, patchouli, stevia, citronella, cinnamon, areca nut, orange, pineapple, grapes, large cardamom, *safed* musli, plum, pear, peach, walnut, geranium, and tomato.

In the field of horticulture West Siang district has its own mark of distinction. Fruits growers from West Siang have bagged many prizes in different exhibitions and competitions; and also supplied their horticultural produces in different places. As early as 1968, papaya and pineapple grown in Aalo were considered best in Assam Agricultural Exhibitions. (NEFA Information, 1968, 2 (8): 18-19). This apart, the first fruit processing industry, namely, Arunachal Horticultural Processing Industries Limited (AHPIL), was set up at Nigmoi near Aalo which began commercial production with effect from 1st October 1987. (Ete, 1999: 38-41). This fruit processing unit was started because of large scale production of pineapples and oranges in the area. It is therefore reported in 1979 that Basar was the nerve centre of pineapples with the potentiality of having a fruit processing plant. (Hazarika, 1979:15). The abundance of fruits production which led to the setting of AHPIL can be gauged from the fact that Agricultural Farm at Aalo had started producing jam, jelly and squash from November-December 1979. (Arunachal News, 1980:38).

Before 1980s horticultural activities were undertaken in a small scale. As on 31st March 1973, 10 people's horticulture garden and 1 horticultural nursery were recorded for West Siang district. (GoAP, 1972-73: 56). But in 1980s the activities intensified. In 1984-85, 100 acres of land were reported under horticultural garden. In 1986-87 and 1987-88, 18 acres under people's horticultural garden for each year have been covered. In 1987-88 also, 180 acres and 164 acres were brought under command area plantation and vegetable gardens respectively. During the year of reference, in 7 Galo inhabited circles, 367 people's horticultural gardens were reported. However, in the district as a whole 6522 MT of temperate and tropical fruits were recorded produced in 1923.60 ha. (GoAP, 1988:36-37). In 1988-89, 17 acres under people's horticulture garden, 201.39 acres under compact horticultural garden and 136 acres under vegetable gardens were recorded. During the year of reference, 25,770 fruit plants were distributed and 12,000 old plants rejuvenated. (AoPs, 1984-85, 1986-87, 1987-88 and 1988-89). During the year 2007-08, in 7 Galo inhabited circles in the district 763 horticultural farms and nurseries were reported under Technology Mission and 115 under Bamboo Mission. For the district as a whole 22,485.83 MT of temperate fruits like apple, pears and plums and sub-tropical fruits like orange, guava, pineapple, banana, litchi, large cardamom were produced in 5022 ha of land. The production of fruits like apple, pears, guava, pineapple, and litchi in 2007-08 has spectacularly declined as compared to 1987-88. However, the production of orange has gone up from 1002.80 ha to 2698 ha with corresponding production from 1150 MT to 8632 MT.

Before commercial fruits were introduced, as has been mentioned, the Galo people used to plant jackfruit trees and *buyu* (local banana). In 1946 the practice of growing bamboos and jackfruit trees was recorded in Yomcha area and of potatoes and red pepper in Daring village[21].

Horticultural activities were undertaken by the department of agriculture during initial period of the development intervention. Since then Galo area has attracted the attention of the planners for the development of horticultural activities. This is quite evident from our foregoing discussions. But the available records with the Department of Horticulture show that 10 out of 16 sample villages in West Siang were provided with different schemes under horticulture. During field study the researcher came across some horticultural gardens in the above five villages. Some of the gardens were raised by people themselves. For example, in Siru Mr. Tajum Kamum has planted banana and pear in his *lugo* (compound garden). But in other villages there are uncared orange gardens[22]. Though there are horticultural gardens under government schemes, the researcher also found gardens raised by few individual families through self initiatives in villages like Kabu, Darka, Piri, etc.

In Chekor Lombi 14 beneficiaries were recorded in 2 years from 2002-03 to 2004-05 under Technology Mission. They were provided with 15 schemes (number of a scheme has been shown in parenthesis) such as cardamom (3), pineapple (1), organic manure (1), tunnel (1), orange (5), vegetable (1) and ginger (3). One beneficiary was recorded under two schemes. In 2006-07, only one beneficiary was recorded under orange scheme. Beside Technology Mission, 3 beneficiaries each under SGSY and Bamboo Mission were recorded. Under SGSY the 3 beneficiaries had availed of the scheme on ginger cultivation.

In other 9 villages, 167 beneficiaries were recorded against 215 numbers in 21 schemes under Technology Mission. The difference between the number of beneficiary and number of scheme tells that a single beneficiary has availed of more than one scheme. For example, in Kabu 6 beneficiaries have availed of the same scheme twice, while 1 beneficiary availed 4 schemes in 4 years. The records also show that 1 beneficiary had got three different schemes in the same year. The records also reveal that in remote villages the instance of 2 or more schemes against one beneficiary is either 0 or very rare. For example, in Lite Boje and Siru Tali, no beneficiary has availed of 2 or more schemes. In each of Ringi and Piri villages, there is only 1 beneficiary with 2 schemes. In Kabu and Tadin, there are 10 and 9 beneficiaries respectively with 2 or more schemes.

The schemes and beneficiaries (shown in the parenthesis) in each scheme under Technology Mission in 9 villages include organic manure (4), floriculture (6), litchi (1), vegetables (10), black pepper (2), pineapple (11), manually operated tools (18), medicine (8), orange (69), ginger (8), guava (1), cardamom (19), potato (3), banana (6), citronella (19), earth worm (2), aromatic plant (28), water tank (1), cinnamon (1), walnut (2), and low cost tunnel (1). It was observed that citronella grass was provided under aromatic plants and the schemes whether citronella or aromatic plants were availed by many beneficiaries only for subsidy. Though West Siang is famous for pineapple the number of schemes in 9 villages are only 11 against 69 schemes of orange cultivation. Litchi, cinnamon, guava, and walnut schemes are not as popular as can be deduced from the numbers recorded.

The schemes discussed here are recorded from 2001-02 to 2006-07. But for all the villages except Kabu, Darka, and Liru, the beneficiaries are not recorded for all these years. For example, in Lite Boje and Siru Tali, the schemes were provided only during one year, namely 2004-05. In Piri, it is 2 years from 2002-03 to 2004-05.

Horticulture has also been developed under Bamboo Mission and SGSY programme. However, all the villages are not found benefited. There are 11 beneficiaries listed under Bamboo Mission only for the year 2007-08 in Darka, Chekor Lombi, Kabu, Tadin and Piri. Under SGSY programme 7 beneficiaries (number against the scheme is shown in parenthesis) were found recorded under banana (3), pineapple (1), orange (2), and ginger (1) in Paya, Siru Tali, Tadin, Piri, and Darka between the period 2007-08 and 2009-10.

The resources used for development of horticulture to provide money income to the farmers has not been realised in many villages. For example, in Siru, Piri and Siru Tali, pears have become the fodder of pigs as they could not be marketed. Because of their distance from the market, head load of transport becomes very difficult. People rather prefer vegetable crops to fruits crops as a head load of vegetable weighs less than that of fruits. The people who have enough jhum land have converted it to horticultural fields. In Piri, jhum lands have been converted to horticultural land. In Lite Boje in 1977 *rebab* (a citrus fruit) saplings were supplied for orange saplings.

A similar case was reported in Tapo where banana stumps provided for the garden were found to be of wild varieties. In villages like Paya, Tadin and Piri, a few beneficiaries recorded against the village actually do not belong to the village. In Tadin there is no bamboo plantation and it has become a failure in Kabu. In Lite Boje, however, there are natural bamboo groves. One common trend which was reported is that a number of schemes availed are not actually implemented. In villages nearer to urban centre one beneficiary has got many schemes because of political connection whereas in interior villages there are not diversified schemes like those in exposed villages. Interestingly, in villages like Piri, Ringi, and Siru many people have started their own horticultural gardens. The citronella schemes are not popular though there are quite a good number of beneficiaries. The beneficiaries of citronella and aromatic plants practically did not implement the scheme as they did not have an easy market nearby. The same is the problem with cardamom scheme in Darka. It was reported that the beneficiaries in remote villages use ash and kerosene for disease control while in exposed villages pesticides are used. A case of intensive land use practice was also observed in Kabu where a beneficiary benefits from two schemes—Apna Van and cardamom-on the same land.

Under Hariyali programme[23], out of 15 study villages there are only 10 beneficiaries recorded against banana scheme (2), bamboo plantation (1), and cardamom plantation (1) in 2008 and another 6 cardamom plantations in 2007 only in Darka village. From field study it was found that Hariyali programme was not launched so far in other study villages, though, the programme is popular in many villages like Basar, Kugi, Gune Bane, Bopak, Biru, etc.

Fisheries

Fisheries development started in the state in 1958-59 with two schemes, one of which is an opening of a Community Fish Farm at Kabu near Along. (Anon., 1979:17). Obviously, West Siang district was also the first beneficiary in fisheries development. Subsequently, intensive development of fisheries sponsored by the Ministry of Food and Agriculture was taken up in Along area (GoI (NEFA), 1965-66:7) of present West Siang district. As per available records 3 People's Fish Farms were recorded in 1972-73 (GoAP, 1972-73:62) which rouse to 5 in 1981 (Dutta Choudhury, 1994:160) and to 30 in 1987-88 (GoAP, 1986-87 & 1987-88: 31) in West Siang district. Further village fish ponds were recorded 307 in 1972-73 (op cit. 1972-73) which rose to 339 in 1987-88 (op cit. 1986-87 & 1987-88) during a period of 15 years. But during 2003-04 (GoAP, 2003-04:78) only 30 people's fish ponds were found recorded. Again as on 31st March, 2007 village fish ponds have dropped to 10. (GoAP, 2003-04:78).

Though there is inconsistency in data, still government initiative through introduction of schemes for fisheries development in the district, predominantly inhabited by the Galo people, is evident. Under fisheries development programme the Department of Fisheries, Arunachal Pradesh, has incurred an expenditure of Rs 242.14 lakhs in 2006-7 (₹ 2.6 Lakhs for West Siang District) and ₹ 278.0 lakhs in 2007-08 towards administration, maintenance, and training and extension programmes for the state as a whole.

During the period of 13 years from 1995 to 2007 a total of 254 beneficiaries have been recorded in nine years under rural aquaculture and Fish Farmer's Development Agency (FFDA) programmes in West Siang District. From 15 sample villages there are 22 beneficiaries (shown in parenthesis against the village) in 6 villages namely, Paya (6), Darka (5), Kabu (5), Liru (2), Lite Boje (2) and Chekor Lombi (2). Of these 6 villages, Darka, Liru, Paya and Kabu are nearer to administrative headquarters while Lite Boje and Chekor Lombi are well communicated. In other villages, the researcher found small size of land holdings in river beds which are used for WRC. Because of less plains land due to hilly region, these 9 villages do not have fish ponds. In one of the villages namely Ringi, the researcher was reported, "Fishes are available in plenty in the river"[24]. In 6 villages with fish ponds the researcher has interesting experiences. In Paya one of the fish ponds, which was earlier a WRC field, was reverted to the same again. One beneficiary who has a pond at a distance from the village does not take care due to his other engagement and stealing of fishes. Only one beneficiary is found properly maintaining the fish pond.

The general impression in all the villages is that people opt for the scheme to get the benefit of subsidy. That is why in the villages either fish ponds are left uncared or do not exist.

The government programmes and achievements have macro perspectives with micro variations across villages. Each sample village provides a different picture of land resource management while pursuing agricultural and allied activities.

Forestry in West Siang

The forests of West Siang district have also been classified according to their legal status. Under wildlife sanctuary there are two wildlife sanctuaries, namely Kane Wildlife Sanctuary, notified in 1991 and Yordi-Rabe Supse Wildlife Sanctuary, notified in 1998 and 2007 respectively. The Kane sanctuary covers an area of 55 sq km, the Yordi-Rabe Supse sanctuary covers an area of 496.15 sq km, the reserved forests cover 248.18 sq km and USF 3144.82 sq km making it 3944.15 sq km in total under three legal forest categories. Records of areas on protected forests, Anchal reserve forests, village reserve forests and national parks are not available. The reserved forests are located in Aalo and Likabali forest divisions covering an area of 126.1 sq km and 122.08 sq km respectively. The reserve forests in the districts are in Dipa, Likabali, Libar Hill, Bahadur Hill, Mechuka St/Sf, Rangee, Maru Jaru, Jori Take Pujo, and Echi. Under the scheme of Aided Natural Regeneration, an area of 20 ha each for the years 1996-97 and 1997-98 were covered in West Siang district. Under artificial plantation the achievements were recorded from 1994-95 to 1997-98 and then in 2002-03 and 2005-06. The total area brought under this scheme is 1093 ha. (Shina, 2008, op cit.).

By 31st March 2007 there were seven ranges and nine beats in West Siang district. During the period of reference 75 ha have been brought under regeneration scheme. A total of 500 plants were also raised under avenue plantation and 100 ha under Apna Van scheme in Aalo Forest Division. But plantation scheme in Likabali sub-division has been more diversified in the same year than in Aalo sub-division. During the same period of reference 147 ha were brought under afforestation and 278 ha under Added Natural Regeneration scheme. Another 25 ha and 1 ha of plantation were raised under Minimum Needs Programme and others. Further under Apna Van scheme 200 numbers of plants were raised. (GoAP (d), 2007).

Before the Supreme Court's decision in 1996[25] data are available on major forest activities for a period of eight years from 1985-86 to 1994-95. During this period 840.75 ha were planted under various schemes as against 1261 ha of maintenance. (GoAP (d) 1985-86, 1988-89, 1994-95, & 1994-95). Maintenance was given more importance than plantation. In 2002-03, an area of 500 ha was brought under Afforestation and 58 ha under Aided Natural Regeneration in addition to the distribution of 15,000 seedlings. Though data are available in piecemeal the forest activities undertaken were mainly interventions through government schemes. During the period of reference Aalo forest division had earned revenue of ₹ 21,05965 from minor forest products, seized sawn timber and supply of charcoal. (GoAP, 2003-04). No doubt forest activities have been centred around commercial use of forest resources and regeneration for commercial purposes.

The government's commercial interest in forest had two operational dimensions. The government department itself operated forest resources with a commercial motive and later contract was given to local people for such a purpose. Commercial use of forest resources by the local people found a favourable base in the emerging demand for timber and other resources from developmental needs. The offices needed furniture and the schools needed benches and desks. For all these uses wood came from the forest.

In Galo area, Aalo was the district headquarters of the former Abor Hills District from 1st February, 1953 and continued to remain so in Siang Frontier Division and later when West Saing district was renamed and bifurcated in 1965. Moreover, Government Higher Secondary School at Aalo is one of the oldest higher secondary schools in the state. In Galo inhabited area of West Siang district, there were 64 educational institutions by the end of 1970 and 164 by the end of 1987 and by 2002 it increased to 257. (Begi, 2007: 213-217). The furniture requirements of all these schools were met from the forests of Galo area.

Many furniture units came up to meet these requirements. It is to be mentioned that the licence to use forest resources was given to the Galo people who operated sometimes by themselves and more often by engaging outside labourers. The furniture requirements include not only wood works but also cane and bamboo works. Doji (2003) records 9 forest based industries in Along circle (7 in urban centre and 2 in rural area) by 2001, which include wood furniture unit, wood carving unit, cane and bamboo product unit, saw mill, veneer and plywood mills.

It is to be further mentioned that the emerging modern elite groups had a taste different from the traditional way of life. Their furniture requirement included sofas, *almirah*, chairs and tables, which were not used in traditional society. They also used sawn timbers to construct Assam type buildings initially.

The development activity after independence had two visible impacts on the demographic pattern. Many people outside Galo area came to work in different capacities both in government and private sectors. Forest areas were cleared to accommodate development projects like office compound, road construction, residential houses for employees, schools, hospitals and market complex. In response to the concentration of development activities in administrative headquarters rural-urban migration took place. There were floating population who came for education, treatment or for official purposes. But there were other villagers who migrated and settled in urban centres. These people demanded bamboo and wood for construction of houses and to meet the fuel needs. There was heavy pressure on the forest resources adjacent to administrative headquarters.

Even the flow of resources from distant rural areas was not altogether absent. As many Galo people lived in administrative headquarters and the forest resource was dwindling, leaves and other vegetables from the distant village forest were sold in the urban market places. The resources used within the village community crossed the village and even district boundaries.

The forest land whether community or privately owned were put to alternative uses. The establishment of Nigmoi food processing unit encouraged horticultural gardens. The demand for citronella also brought forest land under its cultivation. Commercial crops like ginger, mustard, chillies were introduced in forest lands. In recent years plantation crops like tea, kiwi, have been introduced.

Forestry in Sample Villages of West Siang

Out of 16 sample villages, 12 villages were benefited under Apna Van scheme as per available records. Normally, each beneficiary got 1 ha under Apna Van scheme except a few in Darka and Kabu villages. In Kabu, there are 4 beneficiaries with 3 ha and 6 beneficiaries with 2 ha under the scheme. In Darka, there are 3 beneficiaries with 2 ha, 1 beneficiary with 5 ha and 1 beneficiary with 4 ha of land covered under this scheme. The scheme started in 1997-98. But from that year till 2007-08, no beneficiaries under the said scheme have been recorded against any of the sample villages. For example, in Kabu from 1997-98 to 2007-08 only the schemes were recorded for 6 years. During the period of 6 years only 19 beneficiaries were assisted under Apna Van scheme, out of which two beneficiaries have availed the scheme twice each.

In Darka, for a period of 5 years from 1997-98 to 2006-07, there were 31 beneficiaries assisted as per records available and 1 beneficiary was found having been assisted twice. In Paya for a period of 3 years from 1997-98 to 2006-07, only 5 beneficiaries were assisted. In Yiga, Ratak Gamlin, Chekor Lombi and Tapo, only 1 beneficiary is recorded in each of the village. In Lite Boje, in 3 years from 1997-98 to 2006-07, there are three beneficiaries with 1 beneficiary availing the scheme twice. In Siru Tali in 1997-98 and 1998-99, 2 beneficiaries were recorded under the scheme. Similarly, in Tadin there were two beneficiaries in 1997-98 and 1 in 2006-07. The case of 4 beneficiaries has been recorded in 1997-98 in Siru village. As per records there is no continuity of assisting beneficiaries in every village except Siru Tali in every year during the period from 1997-98 to 2007-08. In initial years number of villages assisted was 10 which subsequently declined village wise and beneficiary wise.

During field study the enthusiasm of the Galos for raising Apna Van was noticed by the researcher. In Tapo, long before the Apna Van scheme was introduced, an individual was reported having planted commercial timbers in his land. Later in 1997 this was recorded under Apna Van scheme. During field study in July 2010, it was reported that the trees are around 25 years old or more. It was also reported that the son of the beneficiary has planted *hollock* by the side of the earlier plantation of the father. In Paya and Tadin the plantation actually started after the scheme as the trees looked very young, about 5-7 years old. In Tadin, it was also reported that the beneficiary has raised Apna Van about 20 kms away from the settlement area. The beneficiary is assisted for 1 ha of land, whereas, he along with 3 other members from the village, has planted in more than 2 ha of land.

In Lite Boje a case was reported where the seeds supplied were exotic varieties and the trees did not survive long because of disease. However, there are a few cases of private plantation on self initiative. The exotic varieties are those which are not *hollock* or *hollong*, which the people grow abundantly. In all the cases *hollock* and *hollong* trees are reported sustaining. That is why in Darka and Kabu villages quite a number of private forests of *hollock* and *hollong* trees are found doing well and sustaining. Out of these private forests many were created on self initiatives which were later placed under Apna Van scheme for assistance.

As has been said, in Tadin, the Apna Van is raised in a far away place. Similarly, in Siru Tali, the Apna Van of *hollock* plantation has been created in a far away place bordering the village of Sere Tali. It follows that Apna Van does not interfere with the traditional land use practice; it is an emerging trend of new land use practice. This also points to the fact that natural vegetation is destroyed for creation of Apna Van. Another striking finding during field study is that there is a discrepancy between the name of beneficiary in the record and beneficiary in the village. In a village (name is withheld) as per the record there is 1 beneficiary belonging to that village whereas other beneficiaries are not members in that village. In the same village the researcher did not find any Apna Van though the beneficiary is a member of that village. Later it was found that the beneficiary has settled in another place. Probably, the Apna Van scheme was implemented in his new place of residence. All the schemes implemented in the district were not found in all the villages. In other words all the villages have not been benefited from all types of schemes equally. In this connection it is to be mentioned that the researcher did not find any case of avenue plantation in degraded *jhum* land in any one of the study villages.

Hunting and Foraging

From the very beginning of development interventions tribal people's hunting and fishing practices were well recognised. Even the draft rules to govern hunting and fishing did not include any provisions to control hunting or fishing by the tribal people themselves. However, hunting by officers and officials were put under scrutiny. Nevertheless, it was realised that tribal people should be persuaded to be careful in their hunting pursuits. (Elwin, Shastri & Simon, 1967: 25-27). Except Wildlife Protection regulations, no strategies have been made to regulate hunting practices of the state in general and in Galo areas in particular. No distinction has been made on hunting relating to culture and dietary supplement, and market demand and pastime.

However, it was observed that hunting is no more an important source to supplement the diet in Galo villages. Further, its ritualistic significance was reported declining. During field study, from discussions with Galo intellectuals and villagers, the researcher was enlightened of the causes of declining ritualistic significance relating to hunting practices.

Two plausible causes were forwarded. The first one is concerned with conversion to Christianity. Second, rituals have assumed more of secular characteristic with the spread of education and interaction with people from different communities.

In earlier time, the Galo people almost remained in the village; every one lived like other fellow villagers, and lived as community person following the prescriptions of culture. In body and mind the people were a part of the ritualistic practices and their significance in day-to-day life. But due to education and changing occupational pattern many people stayed away from the traditional life. Though they are traditional, still the impact of tradition has got diluted due to the exposure of the people to diverse traditions. Rituals invariably require taboos and movement restriction which is not possible in many cases in recent times. When a practice interferes with a way of life it gradually declines. That is why many rituals, for example relating to curing of diseases, have declined. In hunting the traditional methods and weapons along with group and community participation have also declined with the availability of guns and occupational diversification. Naturally, rituals associated with traditional techniques of hunting have declined.

In turn individual hunting has become important which has apparently two dimensions. Individual hunters go for hunting to meet requirement of the family or as a pastime. Hunting is not a regular pursuit to these hunters like the expert hunters in the village. For the expert hunters, hunting is like an occupation. They do not only hunt of their own but also go for hunting on the basis of information about prowling of animals from any neighbouring villages. In place of sharing the surplus, meat is sold either in the village or in the market place.

But instances are not rare when hunting is carried out for social considerations. Among the Galos there is a tradition of sending gifts of meat from son-in-law's family to his father-in-law's family[26] and vice-versa. In many families hunting happens to be a source of sending meat of wild animals to relatives. An individual also often hunts to honour his guests, relatives, and friends.

It is a common practice among the Galo to carry a gun whosoever possesses it when going to a forest. Earlier, they normally used to carry *dao*. Carrying a *dao* or recently carrying a gun has more of a security concern than a hunting motive. Traditionally, when the motive is for hunting, the Galo people used to carry hunting equipments along with the *dao* even in individual hunting. But this motive is not discernable when a man carries a gun. If he chances upon an animal or bird he kills it if possible. Such animals are not always distributed or shared as per the traditional norms. Male members of the village, often close kins in big villages, feast on it outside the village[27].

The researcher fortunately was present during her field study from 11th September 2010 to 16th October 2010 when deer, tiger, bear were killed. In her previous field visits she had not chanced upon any case of hunting. Usually, *dichi* (winter) is the hunting season. But the hunting that the researcher chanced upon had taken place in the autumn season. It was informed that at any time in a year a hunter with the gun kills an animal or bird if he finds in the forest.

Traditionally also hunting and trapping were not restricted at any time in a year. One could go for hunting when he feels the like. But the Galo people call winter the hunting season. During this time migratory animals and birds are found in large numbers and people are free from agricultural activities. Winter is the season for marriage, house construction, etc. During marriage large quantity of meat is required which people try to get from hunting. During other times though people used to go for hunting, the number of people involved and frequency of hunting are very low.

When people used to go for hunting traditionally without a gun, they were bound by certain restrictions. Usually, *nyigams* go for hunting more frequently than others. In the past, bow and arrow was used and arrow heads were smeared with poison. Collection, preparation and application of poison used to follow rituals and taboos. Besides, other people were also involved in the process. As iron was not easily available, people were cautious about the shortage of iron made arrow head. Animals and birds were not found in abundance as in winter season and the people would not take risk of uncertainty after rituals, taboos and labour. So, very few people, occasionally, used to go for hunting. On the other hand, trapping was a common practice during these seasons. There were traps for catching big animals also. Hunting with a gun did not require ritualistic restrictions. Hence, the frequency of hunting during 'non-hunting' seasons has increased. The rise in the frequency of hunting however has reduced the frequency of trapping in recent years. Whenever, people go for trapping they lay down traps for small animals only. The practice of trapping big animals has almost stopped.

The disappearance or decline of a practice normally leads to decline and disappearance of technical knowledge about it. When the practice of trapping is gradually declining it is but natural that the knowledge about making the trap and laying it in a right manner will disappear. That is why during interviews all the middle aged and young people in Siru village were recorded having no knowledge in trap making though a few of them purchased traps from outside the village, especially from Aalo[28]. However, the knowledge of its existence will remain in the collective memory of the people for few generations. Needless to say, people remember the tradition of dyeing, some plants used in the process but not the technology. Similarly, people remember the tradition of making *takam pichi* (earthen pot) but not the technology of it.

While the researcher was conducting research in a sample village[29] she was informed about the killing of a tiger in a nearby village. The tiger was a menace to the *mithun* population. When she intended to take a photograph she was denied on the ground that the publication of photo may bring legal problem as tiger is a protected animal. One of the villages in that area had faced problem when an enquiry committee from Ministry of Environment visited that village. But usually the Galo people do not kill a tiger as they believe in a kinship relation. But during her stay at the sample village she learnt that there is no hesitation in recent years to kill a tiger whenever there is an opportunity. If the hunter is a believer in indigenous faith he used to perform rituals after killing the tiger. Though, there was no case reported during field study of a Christian Galo killing a tiger, the researcher from her discussion with the elders came to know that they would not perform the ritual following their Christian tradition. The meat of the tiger is eaten up at the time of the rituals by the male participants. Even to this day women are not permitted to consume the meat of the tiger and for that matter of any stripped animal.

The hide of the tiger was sold overnight at a price of ₹ 60,000/- to a nearby agent. It was also reported that the price of a tiger hide is about ₹ 3 lakhs in neighbouring towns of Assam.

In another village the researcher met a young hunter of around 20 years of age who had killed three bears two days ago. He is a *nyigam*, a recognised hunter in traditional sense. He had earlier information about the locality/habitation of a bear. But he found three bears, one male, one female, and a cub in that locality. He killed three of them with his gun. As the hunter was a Christian he did not perform any ritual after the killing or before going for the hunting. However, he informed the researcher that he had prayed the Lord to protect him from accidents and misfortunes, for 'evil expulsion'. The prayer is ritualised, coined as *kumgurnam,* from the root word *kumnam*, meaning prayer; and is organised in the house of the hunter, but not in the church. It is to be mentioned that the hunters usually perform rituals not only to avoid misfortunes but also to succeed in hunting expedition.

The meat of three bears was distributed in the village and each family got a large quantity which they shared with their other family members, relatives and friends and a few government officials living in different parts of the state. In some families still a large quantity remained which they would preserve through smoked process. The hides were consumed. Usually, the Galo people do not sell the hide. Often they use it in making haversack and small bags.

The tradition of hunting, however, does not exist with same intensity in all the villages. In Siru the old people proudly narrated their hunting expeditions and number of animals killed when they were young. In recent years, owing to old age, they do not go for hunting and members of younger generation have migrated to or frequent urban centres. Their short sojourns in villages do not motivate them for hunting as was traditionally done. Because of their frequenting to urban centres for education or to avail of government schemes, they are not into the traditional way of life in which hunting was an important source of livelihood. Nevertheless, a few of them occasionally go for trapping, or hunting small animals and fishing. There are also a few members of younger generation who live with their parents in Siru village. But they also do not take up hunting as a major subsistence activity.

It is to be mentioned that the mere presence or absence of large number of young people does not determine the intensity of hunting. In the sample village where the bears were killed, the intensity of hunting is more than that of in Siru. In that village, the hunter is the only married[30] young man living with his parents as compared to three married young man in Siru. In both the villages other young men, both married and unmarried, have migrated to urban centres. Usually, people migrate to settle permanently or for a long period to pursue education or job or to stay with relatives.

Foraging like fishing and collection of vegetables among the Galos supplements the dietary requirements. In addition to this, they also collect many other items for different purposes. These items include collection of honey, edible insects, firewood, house building materials, etc. which they use for different purposes.

Traditionally, people did not have any artificial source of fishing. In other words, natural sources like rivers, rivulets, streams, ponds, lakes, and swamps provided the fishing ground. These sources were either community-owned or private owned. Quite for a long time the rivers that flow in the village territory are found to be privately owned. Same is the case with natural ponds, swamps, lakes etc. Though, there was private ownership, more often fishing was done on a community basis. But no individual without permission would go for large scale fishing. In recent years privately owned river segments are leased out for a period that varies from three to five years in different villages. The conditions of lease are also different in different villages.

In Kabu, the privately owned river segments are commonly leased out for a period of three years by Gida-Isi Committee through tender to the highest bidder of the village. Whereas, in Paya, the river segments are given on tender to fishermen from outside by individual owners for a period of five years with the condition that the catch of one year would go to the village fund. In Kabu it is a provision in the tender that the villagers would purchase the fish the price and quantity of which would be fixed by the village committee. But this is not a practice in Paya village. Unlike the earlier practice of sustainable fishing the present practice has become unsustainable due to the large scale fishing and use of non-traditional technology in fishing. Those who get the lease or contract try to catch maximum fish using drag nets which also catches the small fishes. In Siru there are instances of using explosives occasionally by people from other Galo villages and from other communities.

Foraging of vegetables, fire woods, medicinal plants, construction materials and other minor forest products has taken a new form. People do not exclusively depend on foraging to meet vegetable requirement. In study villages it was found that in many families, vegetables are grown or purchased to some extent. Another trend which was observed is the migration of population from the village. Apparently, it follows that the extent of foraging of vegetables especially for own consumption has reduced. But it was found that the quantity of vegetables collected from the forest has not declined. There is a demand of the forest vegetables not only in urban centres in the district but also in capital complex. Processed bamboo shoot and even fresh vegetables are sent to the market of Itanagar and Naharlagun, the twin capital towns of the state, from Aalo. The agent at Aalo collects vegetables from Galo women from different villages, who bring these for sale at Aalo. These vegetables are transported overnight to reach Itanagar/ Naharlagun in the early morning of the following day. The researcher has found women from Paya, Kabu, Tadin, and Darka villages selling vegetables collected from the forest. Even women from Lite Boje were found selling vegetables from the forests at Aalo. As they are from a distant village many a time they sell their items to a middle person.

Development had diversified the fuel requirements. Though quite a number of households in sample villages, especially in category II and III villages, have gas connections, the demand for fire wood in the households and in the village has not declined. The villages become the source of supply to the urban demand. In urban centres the migrant Galos from the villages require fire wood as a matter of their traditional food habit. It is not a surprise therefore, to find traditional huts attached to R.C.C.buildings, both private and government residential ones, for the purpose of kitchen. The demand is more because the households have increased due to migration from a family. This demand has led to a pressure on forest resources unlike the earlier practices. Earlier jhum plots were the major source of supply of firewood due to long fallow period. As the fallow period has reduced the trees do not grow sufficiently to meet the fire wood requirements. Moreover, the jhum cultivation has also been reduced due to terrace and plains cultivation, horticultural gardens and people's engagement in other contract works, government job, etc.

The shortage of supply of firewood from *jhum* land has exerted pressure on forests. Further the firewood requirement was limited to the village needs. In recent years the firewood requirement has extended beyond the village. In other words, the demand for fuel wood has increased to meet the requirements of the village and also of urban centres. The pressure is more in villages connected with roads. In interior villages without any road communication the jhum lands and nearby forests fulfil the firewood requirement without much pressure on forest. Not only firewood there is also demand for *toko (livistonia jengkinsian siana)* leaves for thatch even in urban centres.

There is another trend noticed during field study. Particularly, in villages near urban centres like Kabu, Darka some families purchase firewood from within the village or from outside. On account of the private ownership of forest land free collection of firewood by felling trees is not allowed unlike earlier practices. This is because reduction of trees in the forest, commodification, and market demand for firewood. In this context it is to be mentioned that commodification is associated with the emerging well defined property right regime which was loose in earlier times probably due to well knit kinship relation and abundance of forest resources. The kinship relation has been diluted because of spread of the kin members beyond the village and declining interactions unlike when they lived together in the villages.

It is clear from the analysis that IK is more diluted in villages with more developmental schemes than the remote villages with less number of schemes. With the decline in IK there is a decline in technology. Further two systems are found to have co-existed in study villages. In traditional pursuits there is still the practice of sharing among the community members. But in the production under different schemes the ethics of sharing does not exist. Therefore, horticultural crops, vegetables, etc. produced under different schemes are sold in the markets. Of course, some of the crops are distributed free of cost among near relatives. But this does not corroborate to the traditional ethics of sharing. It is because these crops are also supplied free of cost to people belonging to outside the village community.

NOTES

1. Archive serial no. 2083/1951, bundle No. 101-1951-III, pp. 72-73.
2. 1 *pura* (an Assamese unit of land measurement) = 1.32 acres.
3. See various issues of Annual Administrative Reports, (GoI (NEFA); also see Arunachal Pradesh Development Report 2009:195-198.
4. For data on recently grown horticulture fruits and spices in the state see Arunachal Pradesh Development Report 2009: 200-201, 209-210)
5. NEFA Information, January 1969, Vol. III, No. 6, p. 19.
6. NEFA Information, January 1968, Vol. II, No. 7, pp. 34-35.
7. NEFA Information, January 1970, Vol. IV, No. 6, p.24.
8. By 1954 plums and *lichis* were produced in agricultural farm at Basar. (see Tour Diary of C Wati Aier, Base Superintendent, Siang Frontier Division, Along, Archival file No-22/55, Archive, Itanagar).

9. See NEFA Information, March 1968, Vol. II, No. 8, pp. 18-19 and Arunachal News, January-February, 1977, Vol. 5, No.9, p.8.
10. For example, the crops grown during 2010 in Belo, a remote village are: *yali, yapu* and *yabar* (paddy varieties); *meku, talar, mebe, peyak, elak, ingin, enge, tape- pedi* and *pete, tanyak, adi peren, namdu, tayak, tami, tay, giyi- yiger, tede, yite; take, baka, yaluk, kope/kasia baka, pumpa, chugri, ujuk, sa, kopak, bayom.* Similarly, in Kabu, the village nearest to district headquarters, the cereal and vegetable crops grown during the same year are: *dane, bali* and *anker* (paddy varities); *meku, talar, elak, ingin, enyo, tepe, adi peren, giyi, take, bak, yaluk, kope, beans, talap, olap,* raddish, cauliflower, cabbage, carrot, potato, *kopak,* coriander, *ujuk, bayom*, ladies finger, lettuce, papaya, *jika.*
11. Based on the information of Shri. Hitum Loya, age around 75 years, village Kabu (now settled at Aalo) on 8/10/2010.
12. Interview with Mr. Bare Tasso, Head Gaon Burha since 1962, around 90 years of age, village Tadin on 1st October 2010. He informed that the villagers opened up the WRC with irrigation channel in the land of Mr. B. Padu. By that time as per his information Kabu and some nearby villages had already started WRC with irrigation facilities.
13. Arunachal News August 1979, Vol.8, No.5, p.60.
14. Arunachal News, June-July 1978, Vol.7, No.3, pp.36-37.
15. Arunachal News, August 1976, Vol. 5, No.5, p-50 and Arunachal News, October 1978, Vol.7, No. 6, p. 47.
16. Kate M.I.P, was commissioned in 1975 from which the fields of Lite Boje were to be irrigated. But due to wrong formation cutting of a distance of 5 km in the canal, the project became a failure.
17. Archive serial no. 2084/1951, bundle No. 101-1951-III, p.135.
18. Archive serial no. 2083/1951, bundle. No. 101-1951-III, p. 75.
19. It is not always that people use chemical fertilizers. There is an instance of soil treatment with aldin dust. Shri. Karto Loya of Kabu village did not apply any manure or fertilizers but harvested bumper potato by treating the soil with aldin dust on the basis of the briefings from technical personnel. (Arunachal News, February-March 1978, Vol. 7, No.1, pp. 40-41).
20. Tour diary of Shri. L.R.N. Srivastava, Assistant Research Officer, Siang Frontier Division, Along. Memo No. SG/RES/9/36.
21. Tour diary of P.L.S. James, A.P.O, Siang Valley Sub-Agency, August-December 1946. File No. Report 13/45, pp.39 & 42.
22. For example in Tapo, an orange garden which was provided under government scheme was found uncared for during field study.
23. Hariyali covers different schemes for afforestation including the

schemes under micro watershed project, and horticultural development.

24. In Tapo village, the researcher was reported about the abundance of fish in rivers. During field study she was reported that the villagers had caught about 200 kg of fish from Ego river using *hipe* method in November 2008.
25. On December, 12, 1996 the Supreme Court passed its historic judgement on the 1995 Civil writ petition No. 202, filed by T.N. Godavarman Thirumulpad against the Union of India and others. The subject matter of the petition was on the cutting of trees and deforestation in the states of Jammu and Kashmir and Tamil Nadu, on which the Supreme Court put a ban. Later, in the same month, the ban order was extended to include Northeastern states.
26. Son-in-law's family has a broader meaning. It does not mean the family of the son-in-law, but it includes all his consanguinal and affinal relatives. Sending of meat has two implications. It could be a general type of exchange or a type of deferred reciprocation. The exchange is general type when the recipient family does not reciprocate or is not in a position to reciprocate. As the gift is associated with prestige and status, every family tries to reciprocate it. The recipient family reciprocates the gift immediately or in some future date.
27. This was learnt by the researcher in Darka village, when she was conducting field study on 6/10/2010. A young man had killed a deer while he was working in the forest. Many young people rushed to the spot and enjoyed the meat. The game animal was not brought to the village and not shared with relatives. Though the reason of the recent trend was not clear, the researcher gained from the discussion that it has a relation with Wildlife Protection Act.
28. In place of decline in traditional knowledge of making traps there has emerged a commercial trend which would preserve the knowledge but is beyond the community. IKS is a community concern. But it needs to be further investigated if the knowledge that was with the community is transected to the community through market forces could be taken as indigenous or people's knowledge.
29. The name of the village is kept confidential at the request of the villagers.
30. The marital status is emphasised because the mobility of the married young men is very less as compared to bachelors.

VI
Summary and Conclusions

In recent development discourse the emphasis is on sustainability, people's participation and precisely on decentralised strategies of development. Therefore, the contemporary academic pursuits have been focusing on development studies in broad or specialised thematic perspectives. The fact of the matter is that development studies are no more discipline-centric; it has evolved into broad, comprehensive and inter-disciplinary areas of inquiry. In contemporary development ideology what is striking is recognition to the significance of IKS as a strategy for sustainable and participatory development, the development that is inclusive. Sustainability is essentially a present resource management strategy so that the future generation is not deprived of the use of resources.

Recent emphasis on IKS comes after the recognition to culture as an enabling agent in development strategy. It is to be mentioned that in early years of development interventions culture did not figure in policies and strategies. Obviously, IKS remained conspicuously absent in development discourse. In fact, the realisation of the significance of ecology in development of people had not dawned at international level and even to developing countries till the Stockholm Conference of the UNO in June 1972. The realisation, however, remained at ideological level for almost a decade and half. Practically, in response to Brundtland Commission Report 1986, Indigenous Knowledge System (IKS) has been emphasised as one of the strategies of sustainable resource management for sustainable development.

Early approaches to development not only ignored IKS but made use of scientific knowledge as an alternative. In other words, IKS was not only ignored but also situated side by side another knowledge system, which basically contradicts the logic of IK. The fact of the matter is that, scientific knowledge has universal application, whereas the universality of IK is community specific and institutionalised in traditions and customs.

With this backdrop, the present research topic was conceptualised to examine the implication of IKS in sustainable resource use and management in relation to development interventions. The research issues were addressed in a cultural context and for the purpose, Galo tribe of Arunachal Pradesh was selected as case study.

Topical Perspectives of the Study

The study is organised into six chapters, but here we present a general perspective on the analysis and findings concerning the research topic.

As awareness of the value of IK to sustainable development has grown, importance of such knowledge in contemporary development pursuits has been greatly recognised. But IK belongs to the people, and therefore an appreciation of people's perspective in resource management is of greater significance. Needless to say, the discussion on IK has been taken up from people's perspective within the frame of worldviews, the mental frameworks that define how people understand their relationship with society and natural environment. Obviously, the Galo worldview of resources, their origin and management has been stressed and this provides the basis for subsequent topical analysis.

Galos have their own perspective while conceptualising resources. They have categorised the resources they use as *kode*-land, *motum*-forest and *isi*-water. But their uses define human-nature and supernature relationship. Obviously, resources to Galo people are not mere means of fulfilling material needs; these also provide a base to understand the non-material aspects, in particular faiths and beliefs, of their culture. Needless to say, the range of uses of the resources has both material and mental significance.

As has been mentioned the resources are used and managed by the Galos in cultural perspective and hence each and every activity related to resource use presents the characteristic of embeddedness in the domain of culture. This theoreticaql perspective has been explained by discussing the contours of resource use, though separately, but without undermining the holistic nature of IK, for the knowledge and value are inseparable and woven together primarily by spiritual and religious ideas that define the human behaviour in cultural perspective.

The use of resources include technology which are culture specific in terms of associated customs, traditions, ethics, values, norms of the community along with the ecological setting of the habitation. In response to interventions both the technology and the perspectives of people change. This theoretical understanding provides the deductive reasoning for a scientific enquiry into the dynamics of the technical knowledge system of the Galo people which they employ in their day-to-day life in the process of resource utilization

For the development of tribal people resources which they traditionally used remained at the core in the development process. It also influences policies and programmes. Necessarily, the Galos did not remain isolated in the process. Their traditional resource base got a new meaning through planned interventions; the resources were used for both subsistence and commercial purposes. In fact they have been experiencing development interventions in various fields since the beginning of the planning period from 1952. The interventions have brought about changes in the nature and context of resource use. In this emerging trend the issue of traditional ethics and values in the sustainable use of these resources has been appreciated. One of the characteristic of this new trend has been the emergence of the regime of private property in place of earlier lineage/clan/community ownership.

Intervention has not always been an achiever. It is greatly related to the acceptability by the people and its compatibility with internal dynamics. The fish culture introduced among the Galos in this regard is a case to the point. The Galo people have been fishing from natural sources and till date fishes are available adequately to meet their requirements. Moreover, fish culture is quite a new area of activity for them as compared to agricultural and horticultural activities. As a result schemes under fisheries have not been proved to be successful as compared to schemes under agriculture and horticulture.

Further, intervention quite often impacts the traditional relations in any field the forestry in Galo area provides an example when the traditional relation between Galos and their forest use got redefined. The new relation became visible through commercial interests in forest use and expansion of government control over forests which earlier belonged to the community.

Resources in traditional communities were used for subsistence livelihood. The scale of resource use being limited and sustainable, there was no visible pressure on resources so as to reduce it to a critical condition. But policies and programmes directly and through inter-related forces diversified and diverted resource use to commercial purposes linking to market for money. So more land resources were brought under use, forest resources were used more than required for the village community and water resource for fishing was used beyond holding capacity. But in some villages the traditional moorings are still strong; subsistence attitude is still dominant. So people did not bother much when schemes failed or they did not take care of schemes properly, for the end result could not be perceived lucrative as compared to the efforts to be made to achieve the result. Infact the loss by not making the scheme successful was not perceived as a loss. So in that case we can say that the schemes are being used unproductively.

The security aspects with the schemes were not well perceived. So people used resources required for schemes and also to meet the subsistence needs. In between, whatever could be perceived by the people were utilised for commercial purposes. That is why in some villages even without government schemes the people's endeavour was directed towards non-traditional resource use like land use for horticultural purposes.

Status of Indigenous Knowledge System

The study has not only presented Galo world view of resource management in the tradition, but also has discussed the status of IKS in resource management in the contemporary period. Its status in policy and programmes has also been delineated. What is noticed is a decline in IKS in general and an emerging two spheres of activities in particular. In one sphere the tradition is predominant, while in other the scientific system is emerging rapidly. The study also has raised various issues on the basis of the findings during field study.

For example, IK, as has been mentioned, believes in sharing and the practice still continues to a perceptible extent. Fishing in individual owned river segment is not restricted to the community members even today. Of course, the trend of fishing for market has emerged. When market will be predominant, naturally accumulation will replace community sharing. Will then IKS remain as community perspective in the changing situation?

The status of IKS varies in villages with schemes and without schemes. Under the agricultural policy all the study villages have not adopted WRC/TRC. In Siru and Belo all the farmers practise *jhum* cultivation while in other villages both *jhum* and WRC co-exist. There are also cases when beneficiaries under different schemes are mainly from elite groups and few in number. In other words, under a particular scheme neither all the villages nor the families in a village are equally benefited. The status of IKS in those villages and families, where traditional livelihood activities are predominant, has not changed as much as in others. To put logically, the intensity of development interventions is inversely related to the use of IK. But the proposition is not a simple explanation of the emerging reality of the relationship between development interventions and the status of IK.

IK exists in traditional practices, in many cases as a

ceremonial piety. As a matter of tradition they follow the customs and practices, though a few cases have been reported in which people have cast doubt or have modified what they earlier used to practise. But this change is not related to policies and programmes alone; there are influences of religious conversions and other external dynamics. That is why a Christian hunter observes *kumgurnam* in the line of the traditional ritual. In same activities people follow two practices simultaneously. For example, a farmer uses fertilisers and pesticides in terrace and plains cultivation but not in *jhum*.

Nature of Government Interventions

Early policies and programmes were primarily promoting scientific knowledge. So, even when IK was prescribed for the development of the tribals in tribal *panchsheel*, it was practically ignored. Instead of modernising traditional agricultural practices alternatives were introduced along with supply of HYV seeds, controlling *jhums,* and linking traditional sharing economy with the market.

People's engagement with IKS is a long and old experience. With such a long period of pursuits a shift of schemes in short duration does not capture the community imagination in general. So, government interventions through various schemes have not been able to dissociate people from their practice of IKS in traditional livelihood pursuits. That is why the beneficiaries in most of the cases have shown interest in subsidy that goes with the scheme. This long period of association with the knowledge system has provided an outlook and shaped the perception of the people which the shifting schemes of short period duration do not. In spite of concerted efforts by the government the people are still tradition bound, though they are integrated to the forces of development in varying degrees. It would not be out of context to mention that security concern is associated with their traditional outlook. That is why people have not been able to appreciate livelihood security in government schemes with the same level of confidence.

The programmes have been selective and as has been

mentioned, have not covered al families and all villages equally. Through programmes and schemes, non-traditional practices and technology like WRC, fertilisers, pesticides HYV seeds, etc. have been introduced. On the other hand, people have their own perception of the whole process of development interventions.

In recent decades, however, the plan programmes emphasise on social capital and thus on the creation of community consciousness in the process of participation. The community which people had in the tradition and the institutional setup which evolved over the centuries to sustain and maintain such community feeling are not present in the transplantation of community consciousness through development programmes. So, people who still have anchoring in tradition find the community concern through development strategy superficial and, therefore, show a general indifference.

The use of IKS in the production process supports the level of production which is compatible to a subsistence level. An alternative to IKS exists in the production process in the form of use of better technology. Fishing can be done using traditional technology and explosives. When supply of fish is related to the market, certainly, fishing with the use of blasting would be preferred as an efficient alternative to the IKS. In this context two inter-related issues emerge. These are:

- Will ITK with smaller return survive when better technology with a high return to meet the market demand is available?
- Will IK be compatible to a market demand base for a large scale production with a competitive environment and availability of better technology?

Policy Implications

IKS, as has been said, conceptually and meaningfully is consistent with subsistence level of livelihood. On the other hand, application of scientific knowledge in development process aims at securing maximum material prosperity.

Obviously, there is a tension between development strategy aiming at higher level of growth and incorporation of IK into them. In order to handle such a tension there is no provision of institutional set up in policy options. The set up that exists is in the line of formulating and implementing development schemes on the basis of scientific knowledge. Therefore, institutional tools and resources are primary concern for integrating IKS into market linked development strategies. Further, the integration of IK and scientific knowledge with market-oriented development process requires proper management and capacity building of policy makers and managers. In other words, before implementing developmental schemes the prerequisite should be an enabling institutional set up and understanding of the management of resources through IK in a broader perspective. In this context, emphasis should be laid on cultural perspectives across the political, social and economic dimensions of IKS and resource management pertaining to diverse local conditions. It is because cultural insights are holistic understanding of a micro condition.

IK and resource management would work in the policy process if people's genius is upheld. Without developing the people 'along their own genius', it would not be possible to conserve natural resources through IKS. We have learnt this lesson from the experience when plan interventions and tribal *panchsheel* coexisted. Tribal *panchsheel* and development process had different footing during the period from 1959 to 1980s when the significance of IKS in development strategy was realised. In spite of protecting guidelines in the *panchsheel,* the IK declined consequent upon development interventions.

Achievements in terms of quantitative aggregates should not be taken as an indicator to understand the role of IK in resource management, for an aggregate ignores the micro reality which is diverse and contextual. Alternatively, human well being and vulnerability should be taken into account while integrating IKS, resource management and development policies. Further, there should be clarity on development ideology among the policy makers and development managers while handling the issue of IKS and resource management in development strategies. This calls for our attention as the quantitative information on achievements of development programmes do not reflect any concern for the IK

Primarily, the ideological basis of development has two perspectives. The first one is people's perspective on development which is internal to the community and culture. The other one is macro-perspective on people's development which is external to the community and people. In both perspectives IK in development strategy has different roles to play. In the former, as has been discussed earlier, IKS concerns the community, and the associated level of development is subsistence in nature. In the latter, IKS becomes a commodity of individual concerns, and works towards maximisation of the gain through market linkage. Under such a situation the scientific knowledge, because of its compatibility to development ideology and competitive strength, would marginalise or replace the IK base. There are many empirical evidences to substantiate to the point. Therefore, it is not a surprise to note when people of Siru village purchase traps from the market as they have lost their skill and knowledge of making them in the process of development.

All the above considerations are very much significant before incorporating IKS in resource management vis-à-vis development programmes and policies. Otherwise, IKS and resource management for sustainable development would be more of rhetoric than an objective reality.

Glossary of Terms

Abir	Younger brother (*yame*)/sister (*nyijir*)
Abo Tani	Forefather of Human in Galo belief.
Abo	Father
Achi	Elder brother
Achin	Rice (cooked)
Agi Bagi	A spirit in the form of a rat who found water beneath the ground in Galo myth
Ambin	Rice (uncooked)
Amchi	Roasted rice (*cheera*)
Amo	Paddy
Amtir	Powdered rice
Anam	Smoking
Ane	Mother
An	Leaves
Anyi	Elder sister
Ayo riga	Term used for jhum plots which is cultivated for three consecutive year
Bago	The portion of the Galo house meant for men folk. The hunting weapons and the heads of wild animals and teeth of wild boars hunted are kept in the *bago* portion after performing ritual.
Banam	roasting
Bango Keba	Inter village decision making body.
Bur Tapu	The master of rivers and aquatic animals who falls in love with *Jaayi Bone*
Deli	Soil i.e., red in colour and has less humus and is not preferred.

Depo	Soil typewhich is dark in colour, has more humus and less pebbles
Dere	Community hall
Dichi	Winter
Didu Kubo	The master of forest
Digo Lura	The place of *Mopin*
Digo Monam	Hunting ritual
Yapom Panam	Hunting ritual
Kaji Pomji	Hunting ritual
Peka Panam	Hunting ritual usually performed by seasoned hunters
Dir tachi	Ritual to ward off famine
Diro-Kibo	The hungry dog or the dog of famine in Galo myth.
Diyi Tami	Daughter of *Mopin* married to Abo Tani.
Doli doga	The spirit associated with pest infestation.
Dolu	Village
Donyi Jilo	The highest priest/shaman in Galo myth.
Donyi Mumsi	Daughter of *Donyi* married to Abo Tani
Donyi	Sun
Donyi-Polo	The Supreme Being, the creator
Dumpu	The deer, in Galo folktale.
E	bamboo
Eni	Bamboo variety
Esap	fishing net
Gapu minam	Ritual performed after killing of tiger to ward off the spirit of tiger. The ritual is also performed in case of occurrence death of an individual, especially unnatural death.
Gida	Singular term for all the land and forest owned by a person/clan/village
Heyak	Fishing rod, the line of which form a noose at one end.
Hibok/Sibok	Group fishing by constructing bunds.
Hibu/sibu	River
Higur	Streams
Hile	Portion of deep water in the river.
Hine	Tree

Hipe	The bunds made in WRC fields.
Hipe/Sipe	Community fishing by constructing bund across the river.
Hirek	Ficus sps. Usually considered the dwelling place of *Yapoms*.
Hiri	Individual hunting place usually a fruit bearing tree which wild animals frequent.
Hom	Cane suspension bridge.
Hurin	Ritual performed by a family for prosperity.
Inbo	The wild cat in Jaayi Bone tale
Ir	Bow
Isi Rike	WRC
Isi	Water
Jaayi Bone	One of the most beautiful lady in Galo folktale who is sought by both *Bur Tapu* and *Didu Kubo.*
Jimi Ane	The creator of all.
Kaji-Pomji	Spirits.
Keba	Socio-political institution
Kimen	Dog used during *Kiruk.*
Kipu	The dog in Galo folktale.
Kiruk	Community or group hunting.
Kobuta	Power tiller
Kode	Land.
Kode-isi	Term used to refer to land, forest and water. Here the term *kode* includes both land and forest.
Kole	A variety of wild banana
Kolu	A variety of wild banana
Kormi	A variety of wild banana
Kumgurnam	Prayer for protection (from disease, misfortune etc.).
Kumnam	Prayer
Laklam	Ritual associated with killing of bear or boar.
Liye-lire	Soil type characterized by presence of mostly stones and pebbles and are suitable for the cultivation of orange and edible roots like sweet potato, arum etc.

Lugo/Lau	Enclosure in the homestead for growing varieties of crops.
Mali Rigi	Sweet potato field.
Mebuk	Gun
Medo/Tale	Sky
Mobi	*Jhum* land with a fallow period ranging from 10-15 years.
Mobom	Field with high moisture content.
Modi	Mountain
Modi/Tump Rike	Jhum field
Modir	Usually vertical land not suitable for human use.
Mohen	Field with less moisture content.
Moki Rigi	Jhum field where early variety of paddy are cultivated. Usually such field are small.
Momen	Land suitable for human use.
Mopin	The giver of grain to human. Festival observed for good harvest.
Moro	*Jhum* plots with a fallow period of more than 15-20 years. It also refers to dense forests.
Mute-munyo	
Nahu/nasu	Granary
Nakum	Hut in field
Nam	House
Nam-rumtum	Family
Nginli penam	Ritual performed during large scale collection of honey.
Ngoi/mene	fish
Nyibu	The ritual specialist/Shaman.
Nyida	Marriage negotiation.
Nyigams	Good hunters/warrior
Nyikok	Person well versed in tradition and history.
Nyinya	Tani's son who is abducted by Doji in Galo myth.
Nyipo	Spirits of women who die during child birth or pregnancy.
Nyote	Tiger

Nyopak-Takar	Leopard
Nyoli, Nyoke, Nyomuk, Nyoji	various species of wild cats.
Omo	Poisoned arrow
Onyor	Plant used as a vegetable, the seed of which is also used to stupefy fish.
Opo	Local beer usually made of rice or millet.
Oso	cane
Paper	Logs piled horizontally in jhum fields to prevent washin away of top soil or soil erosion
Pata	WRC
Patak	Payment made in cash or kind for using someone else's jhum field.
Peka or *Bote-Kate*	God of weapon and bravery.
Pelek	Field used for maize cultivation.
Peta mole	Scare crow.
Pip Roksin	Omen through egg.
Polo	Moon/Months
Pombek	Ritual to appease *Yapom,* the guardian of forest.
Ponu	Folk performance usually led by a leader termed *ponu nyibo*
Pura	A land measurement system used of Assam introduced in the state during early plan period.
Rep-remo	Creeper, the occurance of which indicate the presence of *Yapom* in a tree, field etc.
Rige or *enlik*	Reciprocal labour exchange.
Riglap	Labour exchange on payment in kind or cash.
Rigur	Free labour exchange between the relatives.
Rike	Cultivation Field
Rikman	The first year of jhum cultivation in a plot.
Rosi Tami	The daughter of famine married to Tani.
Sichi/Chichi	The earth.
Sijak Dojak jakrap	The period of earth quakes and landslides in Galo creation myth to level the earth.

Sii Piyir	Bird, the sighting of which indicate the time to start cultivation.
Takam	Clay.
Takom Papuk	Bird, the sighting of which indicate the time to start cultivation.
Tami	Millet
Tanyo	Tiger
Tapen	Bat
Taro or *Taki*	The spirit brother of Tani.
Tasak Rigi	Cotton field
Togu panam	Marriage involving sacrifice of mithuns.
Turi	The ancestor of human
Umnam	boiling
Upuk	arrows
Urom	Ghost
Uyi gelik nam	The disposing off of the figurines made with bamboo shavings during rituals.
Uyi/ Uyu	Spirits
Yabur	Misfortune/ill luck
Yapoms	Spirits of forests, water etc.
Yidum	The sacrificial animal/fowl/egg used in rituals.

Bibliography

Archival Records

Archive (Itanagar) Serial No. 2083/1951, Bundle No. 101-1951-III.

Archive (Itanagar) Serial No. 2084/1951, Bundle No. 101-1951-III.

File No. Report 13/45. Tour Diary of Mr. P.L.S. James, Assistant Political Officer, Siang Valley Sub-Agency, From August 1945 to December 1946.

File No. nil. Tour diary of Sri. L.R.N. Srivastava, Asst. research officer, Siang Frontier Division, Along for the months of December and January 1957. Memo No. SG/RES/9/36, Dated the 23rd August 1957.

File No. 27/55. Tour Diary of C. Wati Aier, Base Superintendent, Siang Frontier Division.

Archival file No-22/55, Archive, Itanagar

File No. 5/51(Arc.). Annual Administration Report for the Abor Hills for the year 1950-51.

File No. 4/51 (Arc.). Annual Administration Report of Abor Hills District of NEFA for the Year 1951-52.

Books and Articles

Adhikary, Ashim Kumar 1984. *Society and Worldview of the Birhor.* Calutta: Anthropological Survey of India.

Bagra, Kenbom 2002. 'Some Aspect of Galo Culture with

Special Reference to West Siang District Arunachal Pradesh'. *MPhil Dissertation, Unpublished,* submitted to AITS, Rajiv Gandhi University, Itanagar.

Bagra, Jombi 2009. 'Interpretation of Women in Patriarchy: A Case Study of Galo'. *MPhil Dissertation, Unpublished,* submitted to AITS, Rajiv Gandhi University, Itanagar.

Barik, S.K, 1998: 'Slopping Watershed Environmental Engineering and Technology (SWEET) – A potential Agricultural Land Technology for Midhill regions of Arunachal Pradesh', in M.C. Behera (ed) Agricultural Modernisation in Eastern Himalayas, Commonwealth Publishers, New Delhi, pp. 113-125.

——2004. 'Achieving Decentralisation and People's Participation in Natural resource Management and Rural Development Programmes- Impact of Globaliation in North-East India'. In M.C. Behera (ed) *Globalisation and Development Dilemm- reflections from North East India.* New Delhi: Mittal Publication. pp. 117-129.

Basar, Jumyir, 2004: 'Resources, Resource Management and Resource Based Economy in Nyigam Village', in Tamo Mibang & M.C Behera (Eds),), 2004: *Dynamics of Tribal Villages in Arunachal Pradesh : Emerging Realities*, Mittal Publications, New Delhi. 125-152.

——2006. 'A Passage to Nyime- Galo Rituals that make a Bride a Wife'. In Tamo Mibang & M.C. Behera (eds) *Marriage and Culture- Reflections from Tribal Societies of Arunachal Pradesh.* New Delhi: Mittal Publication. pp. 289-298.

——2006 (a). 'Galo House as a Cultural Space'. In *Resarun, Journal of Directorate of Research*, Itanagar. Vol.32, pp. 105-118.

——2007. 'Rituals and Taboos in Galo Marriage'. In Tamo Mibang & M.C. Behera (eds) *Marriage in Tribal Societies (Cultural Dynamics and Social Realities).* New Delhi: Bookwell. pp. 195-211.

Begi, Joram 2007. *Education in Arunachal Pradesh Since 1947- constraints, opportunities, initiatives and needs.* New Delhi: Mittal Publications.

Behera, M.C. 1994. *Planning and Socio-Economic Development of the Tribals.* New Delhi: Commonwealth.

——1998-99. *Impact of Orange Cultivation on Traditional Role of Galo Women : A Case Study of Pobdi-Gune Bane Village under Along Circle,* Report on Minor Research Project of UGC submitted to Arunachal University, Department of Tribal Studies, Arunachal University, Doimukh.

——1999. 'Understanding Social Reality in Cultural Perspective with reference to the marriage system of the Galos', Regional seminar of Traditional System-Change and Continuity as in the Adis of East Siang District of Arunachal Pradesh, Vivekananda Kendra Institute of Culture, Guwahati and DPYK, Pasighat, Pasighat, January 15-16,1999.

——2004. 'Shifting Cultivation and Man Nature Relationship: An Ecological Study with Reference to Nishing Tribe of Arunachal Pradesh'. B. Dhar & P.C. Coomar (eds) *Tribes of Arunachal Pradesh, History and Culture.* Delhi: Abhijeet Publication. pp. 85-92.

——2008. 'Understanding Forager Worldview and Changing Ideology of Human-Nature Relationship (A study with reference to Sulung, Nyishi and Khampti Tribes of Arunachal Pradesh in North-East India)'. In P. Mohanty, R.C. Malik and E. Kasi (eds.) *Ethnographic Discourse of the Other: conceptualand methodological issues.* Newcastel: Cambridge Scholars Publishing. pp. 8-38.

——2009. *Foraging Mode of Thought and Forager Sulung's Social Self – A critical insight into the concept of foraging mode of thought,* VDM Verlag Dr.Muller, Deutschland, Germany.

——2009. 'Introduction- Rethinking Globalisation: Putting the Idea of Oceanic Circles into Practice'. In M.C. Behera (ed) *Making Gandhi Relevant: Rural Development in the Context of Globalisation.* New Delhi: Commonwealth. pp. 3-51.

——2010. 'A Note on Dynamics of Human-Nature Relationship of Ecosystem People: The Perspective of Nyishi, Arunachal Pradesh'. *Humankind.* Vol. 4-6, 2008-10. pp. 59-71.

Behera, M.C. & Helina Mantaw 1997. 'Development, Deforestation and the Status of Customary Law: A Study of the Khampti Tribe in Arunachal Pradesh'. *Himalayan*

Paryavaran- the Journal of the Environment Protection Society, Vol. 5, Darjeeling.

Berreman, Gerald D., 1968/2004. 'Ethnography! Method and Product'. In Vinaya K. Srivastava (ed), 2004, *Methodology and Field Work.* New Delhi: Oxford University Press. pp. 157-190.

Bhattacharjee, T.K, 1993. *The Frontier Trail*, Manick Bandyopadhyay, Eminent Printing Works, Calcutta.

Bird, David, N, 1990. 'The Giving Environment: Another perspective on the Economic System of Gatherer- Hunters', *Current Anthropology,* Vol. 31, No. 2 pp. 189-196.

——1992: 'Beyond "The Affluent society": A Culturalist Reformulation', *Current Anthropology*, Vol. 33, pp. 25-47.

Borang, Asham, 1998. 'Jhum Cultivation among the Adis of Arunachal Pradesh and Probable strategies for rehabilitation of Jhum Fallows', in M.C. Behera (ed), *Agricultural Modernisation in Eastern Himalayas*, Commonwealth Publishers, New Delhi, pp. 138-155.

——1999. 'Certain Ethnozoological Aspects of Adi Tribe of Arunachal Pradesh, India'. *Ph.D Thesis submitted to Gauhati University, Gauhati. Unpublished.*

Brundtland Harlen Gro, 1987. *Our Common Future*, U.N. Assembly Proceedings: Sustainable Development, 1987.

Chaudhuri, S.K., D.N. Das, U.K. Sarkar & W.S. Lakra 2008. *Indigenous Knowledge and Policy Issues in Fisheries.* Lucknow: National Bureau of Fish Genetics Resources.

Commoner, Barry, 1971. *The Closing Circle*, Alfred Knopf, New York

Dalton, E.T. 1872. *Descriptive Ethnology of Bengal.* Calcutta: Government Press.

Danda, Ajit K. 1994. 'Shifting Cultivation in North East India'. *Journal of the Indian Anthropological Society.* March-July 1994, No. 1&2. pp. 59-73.

Dasgupta, B.K, 1987. 'A Note on Polyandry among Gallongs: AN Analytical Appraisal' in M.K Raha & Coomer (eds) Polyandry in India. Gian Publishing House, Delhi.

Dasgupta, K. 1963: *An Introduction to Galo Language*, Shillong.

Desai, A.R. "Tribes in Transition", in Desai A.R. (ed), *Rural*

Sociology in India, 1969 (1992 reprint), Popular Prakashan, Bombay, pp. 221-231.

Doji, Jome 2003. 'Problems and Prospects of Small-Scale Industries in Arunachal Pradesh'. *M.Phil Dissertation (Unpublished)* submitted to Arunachal University (presently Rajiv Gandhi University), Itanagar.

——2006. 'Aben kabnam—The Marriage Song in the Galo Community'. In Tamo Mibang & M.C. Behera (eds) *Marriage and Culture- Reflections from Tribal Societies of Arunachal Pradesh.* New Delhi: Mittal Publication. pp. 310-311.

Dunbar, GDS. 1915. 'Abors and Gallongs Part I: notes on certain hill tribes of the Indo-Tibetan border'. *Memoirs of the Asiatic Society of Bengal* 5 (Extra number): 1-86. Calcutta

Dunn, G.W., 1896: Preliminary notes on Miri, Shimla.

Dutta Choudhury, S. 1994. (ed) *Gazetter of India-Arunachal Pradesh, East Siang and West Siang Districts.* Shillong: Gazetter Department, Government of Arunachal Pradesh.

Dutta, D.K. 1997. 'Customary land Tenure Syatem and its Change among the Galos of Arunachal Pradesh' in Behera, M.C. & Roy, N.C. (Eds) *Trends in Agrarian Structure in the Hills of North-East India,* Commonwealth Publishers, New Delhi.

Dutta, P.C. & D.K. Duarah, 1965. *A Peep into Social and Economic condition of the Galong in Arunachal Pradesh,* North-Eastern Affairs, Shillong.

Dutta, P.C. 1976. *Mopin, A Festival of Adi of Arunachal Pradesh.* Itanagar: Directorate of Research, Government of Arunachal Pradesh.

Elwin, V., B. Shastri & I. Simon 1967. *Important Directives on Administration of NEFA.* Shillong: North East Frontier Agency Administration.

Elwin, Verrier. 1958. *Myths of the North-East Frontier of India.* Shillong.

——1959. *A Philosophy for NEFA*, Shillong: Government of Arunachal Pradesh (presently at Itanagar).

——1959 (a). *The Art of the North-East Frontier of India.* Shillong: Government of Arunachal Pradesh.

Eshi, Koge 1998. 'Changing Agrarian Economy of the Galos- A Study of two villages under West Siang Districts of

Arunachal Pradesh'. *MPhil Dissertation, Unpublished,* submitted to AITS, Rajiv Gandhi University, Itanagar.

Ete, Minto 1999. 'Problems and Prospects of Food Processing Industry in Arunachal Pradesh'. *MPhil Dissertation, Unpublished,* submitted to AITS, Rajiv Gandhi University, Itanagar.

Ete, T., 1983 & 1984. Nyibo Agom – *The Sacred Religious Literature of the Adi*, 2 Vols., Along.

——1985. *Nyirmen Okke Banggi*, Along.

FAO 1991. FAO 'Global System for Conservation and Utilization of Plant Genetic Resources'. Progress Report and matters for Decision by the Conference. Rome: FAO.

Gadgil, Madhav & Firket Berkes 1991. 'Traditional Resource Management Systems'. In *Resource Management and Optimization.* Vol. 8, No. 3-4, pp. 127-141.

Gadgil, Madhav & M.D. Subash Chandra 1992. 'Sacred Groves'. In *Indian International Centre Quarterly.* Vol. 19, No. 1-2, pp. 183-187.

Gadgil, Madhav & Ramachandra Guha 1992. *This Fissured land-An Ecological History of India.* Delhi: Oxford University Press.

——1995. *Ecology and Equity- the use and abuse of nature in contemporary India*. New Delhi: Penguine.

Gamlin, Mido 2002. 'Linkages between Forest and Tribes'. *M.Phil Dissertation, Unpublished,* submitted to AITS, Rajiv Gandhi University, Itanagar.

Gibi, Mary 2004. 'Economic Life of the People of Tatamori Village'. In Tamo Mibang & M.C. Behera (eds) *Dynamics of Tribal Villages in Arunahcal Pradesh.* New Delhi: Mittal Publication. pp. 163-190.

Goswami, P.C & P.D. Saikia, 1971: *Problems and Economic Development in Tribal Areas with special reference to Dafla and Gallong Tribes of NEFA*, North-East Research Bulletin, Dibrugarh.

Guha, Ramchandra 2008. *How Much Should a Person Consume? Thinking through the Environment.* New Delhi: Permanent Black. (First Published in 2006).

Gyati, Yapa 2005. 'Common Property Resources and Forest Policy: A Case Study of Talley Valley in Arunachal Pradesh'.

Working Paper Series, No. 05. Omeo Kumar Das Institute of Social Change and development. Guwahati: OKD.

Hazarika, Munien 1979. 'Horticulture...no longer an ides'. In Arunachal News. February-March, 1979, Vol. 8, No. 1, pp. 14-15.

I.U.C.N. 1980/1987. Traditional Conservation and Development. June 1987, Geneva: International Union for Conservation of Nature and Natural Resources.

ICAR 1983. *Shifting Cultivation in north east India.* Shillong : ICAR Research Complex for N.E.H. Region.

ILO 1957. *ILO Convention on Indigenous and Tribal Populations,* 1957 (No. 107). Geneva.

——1989. *ILO Convention on Indigenous and Tribal Peoples,* 1989(No. 169). Geneva: ILO.

Kakki, Murnya 2004. 'Customary laws of Marriage among the Galos'. *MPhil Dissertation, Unpublished,* submitted to AITS, Rajiv Gandhi University, Itanagar.

Karbak, Gomo 2006. ' A Note on Gift Exchanges During marriage in Galo Community'. In Tamo Mibang & M.C. Behera (eds) *Marriage and Culture- Reflections from Tribal Societies of Arunachal Pradesh.* New Delhi: Mittal Publication. pp. 333-342.

—— 2007. 'Changing Trends in Marriage System among the Galo: An Overview'. In Tamo Mibang & M.C. Behera (eds) *Marriage in Tribal Societies (Cultural Dynamics and Social Realities).* New Delhi: Bookwell. pp. 277-284.

Karlo, Rejir 2005. *Emerging Pattern of Tribal Leadership in Arunachal Pradesh.* New Delhi: Commonwealth Publishers.

——2007. 'Role of Village Council *(Keba)* in Marriage Conflict: A Study of the Galo System'. In Tamo Mibang & M.C. Behera (eds) *Marriage in Tribal Societies (Cultural Dynamics and Social Realities).* New Delhi: Bookwell. pp. 195-211.

Khondker, Habibul Haque 2004: 'Glocalization as Globalization: Evolution of a Sociological Concept' *Bangladesh e-Journal of Sociology. Vol. 1. No. 2.* July, 2004.

Koyu, Bahi 2009. 'A Demographic Study of Fertility and Mortality of Galos of Arunachal Pradesh: A Study of Koyu

Village'. *MPhil Dissertation, Unpublished,* submitted to AITS, Rajiv Gandhi University, Itanagar.

Lal, Parmanand & Biman Kumar Das Gupta 1979. *Lower Siang People.* Calcutta: Anthropological Survey of India.

Lollen, Tunge 2004. 'Kombo Village- Looking through History and Legends'. In Tamo Mibang & M.C. Behera (eds) *Dynamics of Tribal Villages in Arunahcal Pradesh.* New Delhi: Mittal Publication. pp. 279-290.

——2006. 'Looking Beyond the Rituals- Symbolic Aspects and their Significance in Pugo Galo Marriage'. In Tamo Mibang & M.C. Behera (eds) *Marriage and Culture- Reflections from Tribal Societies of Arunachal Pradesh.* New Delhi: Mittal Publication. pp. 275-288.

——2007. 'A Study of Symbolism in 100 Select Galo Proverbs'. *MPhil Dissertation, Unpublished,* submitted to AITS, Rajiv Gandhi University, Itanagar.

Loyi, Jommi 2001. 'Aspects of the Social Institution of the Galos (A Case Study of Along Circle in West Siang District, Arunachal Pradesh)'. *MPhil Dissertation, Unpublished,* submitted to AITS, Rajiv Gandhi University, Itanagar.

Mackenzie, A. 1994. *The North East Frontier of India* (reprint), New Delhi: Mittal Publication. First reprint in India in 1979.

Madan, T.N., 1986/2004:"In Pursuit of Anthropology" in Vinay Kumar Srivastava (ed),2004, *Methodology and Field Work*, Oxford University Press, New Delhi, pp. 191-207.

Mibang, Tamo & M.C. Behera (Eds), 2004: *Dynamics of Tribal Villages in Arunachal Pradesh : Emerging Realities,* Mittal Publications, New Delhi.

Mili, Rajiv, Mihin Dollo, Prasanna K. Samal & L. Jitendro Singh 2010. 'Shifting Cultivation in North East India: Transition and Contemporary Issues'. In M.C. Behera & Jumyir Basar (eds) *Interventions and Tribal Development-challenges before Tribes in India in the era of Globalisation.* New Delhi: Serials. pp. 132-158.

NEICSSR 1976/1980. *Shifting Cultivation in North East India.* Shillong: NEICSSR.

Norbu, T., 1997. 'Status of Women; Gallong' in Pandey, B.B

(Edt), *Status of Women in Tribal Society,* Directorate of Research, Itanagar.

Nyori, T, 1993. *History and Culture of the Adis*, Omson Publications, New Delhi.

——1998. 'The Religious Beliefs and Practices of the Adis: A Study with reference to Galos'. In M.C Behera & S.K Chaudhuri, (eds) *Indigenous Faith and Practices of the Tribes of Arunachal Pradesh.* Itanagar: Himalayan Publishers.

Pertin, Otem 2009. *Rethinking Tribal Institutions.* New Delhi: Commonwealth.

Post, Mark W. 2008. 'Nominalization-based constructions in Tibeto-Burman: Synchronic and diachronic perspectives' Paper presented at the Max Planck Institute for Psycholinguistics, Nijmegen, NL, May 16.

——2007. 'A Grammar of Galo'. *PhD Thesis*, submitted to Research Centre for Linguistic Typology, La Trobe University, Melbourne.

——2010. 'Lexical numbers, counting and their cultural uses in Galo'. Paper presented at the *Language and Culture Research Group Meeting*, The Cairns Institute, James Cook University, April 19.

Potom, Pennya 2006. 'Some Aspects of Galo Marriage System-A Study with Reference to *Nyiji-Karka* Group'. In Tamo Mibang & M.C. Behera (eds) *Marriage and Culture- Reflections from Tribal Societies of Arunachal Pradesh.* New Delhi: Mittal Publication. pp. 133-140.

Rai, S.C. and I. Maharana 2004. 'Economic Benefits and Conservation Linkages from Ecotourism Development in the Sikkim Himalaya, India'. In M.C. Behera (ed) *Globalisation and Development Dilemm- reflections from North East India.* New Delhi: Mittal Publication. pp. 131-148.

Ramakrishanan, P.S., 1997. 'Scientific Basis of Traditional Wet Rice Cultivation by North-East Indian Hill Tribes', in M.C. Bhera and N.C. Roy (eds) *Trends in Agrarian Structure in the Hills of North-East India*, Commonwealth Publishers, New Delhi, pp. 233-247.

——1993. *Shifting Agriculture and Sustainable Development: An Interdisciplinary Study from North-Eastern India.* New Delhi: Wiley

Eastern. (First published 1992, MAB Book series, Paris: UNESCO & Carnforth: Parthenon Publishing Group).

Redfield, R. 1953. *The Primitive world and its transformation.* Ithaca: Cornell University Press.

——1962. 'The Primitive Worldview'. In M. P. Redfield, (ed.) *Human Nature and Study of Society: The papers of Robert Redifield.* Chicago: The University of Chicago Press. pp. 269-280.

Riba, Bomchak 2004. 'Chilli Cultivation in Dari Village in West Siang District'. In Tamo Mibang & M.C. Behera (eds) *Dynamics of Tribal Villages in Arunahcal Pradesh.* New Delhi: Mittal Publication. pp. 197-206.

——2009. 'Relevance of Indigenous Knowledge System of the Galo of Arunachal Pradesh for Sustainable Development of Forest Resource'. Ph D Thesis, Unpublished, submitted to Department of Geography, Rajiv Gandhi University, Itanagar.

Riba, Mibi 2006 (a). 'Mopin Festival of the Galos: A study on continuity and change'. *M.Phil Dissertation, Unpublished,* submitted to AITS, Rajiv Gandhi University, Itanagar.

——2006. 'Role of Practitioners in Galo Marriage System – An overview'. In Tamo Mibang & M.C. Behera (eds) *Marriage and Culture- Reflections from Tribal Societies of Arunachal Pradesh.* New Delhi: Mittal Publication. pp. 457-464.

Riba, Tomo 1997. *The Tribals and their changing Environment* (A Case Study of Galos (Adi)) of West Siang District, Arunachal Pradesh, Ph.D thesis submitted to Arunachal University.

——1998. 'Problems and Prospects of Agricultural Modernisation in Arunachal Pradesh (Special Reference to the Galos of West Siang District)'. In M.C.Behera (ed) *Agricultural Modernization in Eastern Himalayas.* New Delhi: Commonwealth. pp. 80-87.

——1998 (a). 'Killing of a Tiger: A Ritualistic Recounting of it among the Galos of West Siang District, Arunachal Pradesh'. In M.C. Behera & S.K. Chaudhuri, (eds) *Indigenous Faith and Practices of the Tribes of Arunachal Pradesh.* Itanagar: Himalayan Publishers.

——2000. 'Galo's Eco-Friendly Ways of Fishing'. In S.C.Tiwari and P.P. Dabral (eds), Natural *Resources:*

Conservation and Management for Mountain Development. Dehradun: International Book Distributors. pp. 553-566.

Riba, Tomo 2003. *The Tribals and Their Changing Environment.* Delhi/Itanagar: Himalayan Publisher.

——2004 (a). 'Reciprocity during House Construction: A Bond of Solidarity Among Galo Society- A Study in Disi Village of West Siang District, Arunachal Pradesh'. In Tamo Mibang & M.C. Behera (eds) *Dynamics of Tribal Villages in Arunahcal Pradesh.* New Delhi: Mittal Publication. pp. 87-102.

——2006. 'Aspects of Entertainments during marriage Celebration (Togu Panam) among the Galos of Arunachal Pradesh'. In Tamo Mibang & M.C. Behera (eds) *Marriage and Culture- Reflections from Tribal Societies of Arunachal Pradesh.* New Delhi: Mittal Publication. pp. 259-274.

Roy Burman, B.K. 1985. 'Issues in Environmental Management Cantering Forest, Role of Tribal Communities'. In *South Asian Anthropologist.* Vol. 6, No.1, pp. 41-48.

Sachchidananda 1989. *Shifting Cultivation in India.* New Delhi: Concept Publishing.

Saikia, S.K. and D.N. Das 2004. 'Rice-Fish Culture and its Potential in Rural Development of Arunachal Pradesh'. In M.C. Behera (ed) *Globalisation and Development Dilemm-reflections from North East India.* New Delhi: Mittal Publication. pp. 235-243.

Sarkar, N, 1987. 'The So-called Polyandry among the Gallongs' in M.K. Raha, P.C. Coomar (eds) *Polyandry in India*, Gian Publishing House, Delhi.

Satapathy, K.K., 1997. 'Watershed Management in Hills', in M.C. Behera and N.C. Roy (eds) *Trends in Agrarian Structure in the Hills of North-East India*, Commonwealth Publishers, New Delhi, pp. 248-264.

Shakespeare, L.W. 1914. *History of Upper Assam*, Upper Burmah and North Eastern Fronteir. London: Mac Millan.

Sharma, B.D. 2003 . *Tribal Development –The Concept and the Frame.* New Delhi: Sahyog Pustak Kuteer (Trust). First edition 1978.

Singh, Arun Kumar 1997. 'Ethnogeography and Traditional Agricultural System of the Apa Tanis of Arunachal Pradesh'. In M.C. Behera & N.C. Roy (eds.) *Trends in*

Agrarian Structure in the Hills of North-East India. New Delhi: Commonwealth. pp. 271-283.

Sinha, G.N. 2008. 'Forest and Forestry in Arunachal Pradesh'. *Information Bulletin,* No.27. Itanagar: State Forests Research Institute.

Srivastava, L.R.N., 1962: *The Gallongs*, Directorate of Research, Government of Arunachal Pradesh, Itanagar.

Sundriyal, R.C. and Jamir, Senti 1999. 'Appropriate technology for soil conserving farming system in north east India'. In: *Proceedings of the seminar on "Watershed management in hilly areas- Problemsand prospects"*, published by North Eastern Regional Institute of Water and Land Management (NERIWALM), Tezpur, Assam. pp. 97-110.

Tatak, Talut, 2004. 'Resource Use and Aspects of conservation Practice in Rumgong Village', in Tamo Mibang and M.C. Behera (eds) *Dynamics of tribal Villages in Arunachal Pradesh: Emerging Realities,* Mittal Publication, New Delhi, pp. 153-162.

United Nations Development Programme (UNDP). 1999. *Human Development Report,* New York: Oxford University Press.

World Bank 1997. 'Knowledge and Skills for the Information Age, The First Meeting of the Mediterranean Development Forum'; Mediterranean Development Forum, URL: *http://www.worldbank.org/html/fpd/technet/mdf/objectiv.htm.*

WSSD 2002. *Sustainable Development: Learning and Perspectives from India*, Draft for Discussion. New Delhi: Center for Environment Education, Ministry of Environment and Forest, Government of India.

Government Records

Annual Reports on the Frontier Tribes of Eastern Bengal and Assam (1905–1911).

Arunachal Pradesh Anchal Forest Reserve (Constitution and Maintenance) Act 1975.

Forest Conservation Act, 1980.

Forest Policy, 1952.

GoAP (a). *Annual Operating Plan* for the years, 1982-83 to 2008-

09. Naharlagun/Itanagar: Government of Arunachal Pradesh, Department of Agriculture.

GoAP (b). *Annual Operating Plans (AOP)* for the years 1981-82 to 2008-09. Itanagar: Department of Fisheries, Government of Arunachal Pradesh.

——(c). *Annual Operating Plan (AOP), Horticulture,* for the years 2005-06 to 2009-2010. Itanagar: Department of Horticulture, Government of Arunachal Pradesh.

——(d). *Annual Operating Plan*, for the years 1985-86 to 2009-2010. Itanagar: Department of Environment & Forests, Government of Arunachal Pradesh.

——nd. *Sixth Five Year Plan*, 1980-85. Itanagar: Planning and Development Department, Government of Arunachal Pradesh.

——nd. (a). *State Report on 12th Quinquennial Livestock Census, 1978-79.* New Itanagar: Directorate of Agriculture, Government of Arunachal Pradesh.

——1972-73. *Statistical Handbook of Arunachal Pradesh.* Shillong: Directorate of Economics and Statistics, Government of Arunachal Pradesh.

——1974-75. *Statistical Hand Book of Arunachal Pradesh, 1974-75.* Shillong: Directorate of Economics and Statistics, Government of Arunachal Pradesh.

——1981. *Twenty Year's Developmental Activities of Arunachal Pradesh Since (1960-61 to 1979-80).* Shillong: Directorate of Economics and Statistics.

——1982. *The Arunachal Pradesh Code*, Vols. I – VIII. Itanagar: Government of Arunachal Pradesh, Law and Judicial Department.

——1988. *Basic Statistics of Arunachal Pradesh (1950-51-1986-87).* Shillong: Directorate of Economics and Statistics.

——1986-87 & 1987-88. *Block Level Statistics of West Siang District.* Along: Office of Deputy Commissioner, Economics and Statistics Branch.

GoI (NEFA). *Annual Administration Report.* Various issues particularly for the years 1962-63, '63-64, '64-65, '65-66, '66-67. Shillong: General Administration Department, NEFA Secretariat.

GoI 1986-87. Report of the Commissioner for Scheduled Castes and Scheduled Tribes, Twenty Eighth Report, 1986-87, New Delhi.

——-(NEFA) 1968. *NEFA, Fourth Five Year Plan.* August 1968. Shillong: Planning and Development Department, NEFA.

——2009. *Arunachal Pradesh Development Report,* New Delhi: Planning Commission, Government of India; published by New Delhi: Academic Foundation.

GoN 1980. *Procedures for Implementing a Village wise Approach to Community Development Schemes in Nagaland.* Kohima: Department of R.D. Blocks, Government of Nagaland.

Indian Forest Act, 1927.

News Papers and Other Publications

Arunachal News 1976. 'Report from Districts'. August 1976, Vol. V, No. 5.

——1977. 'Report from Districts'. January-February 1977, Vol. V, No. 9.

——1978. 'Report from Districts'. February-March 1978, Vol. VII, No. 1; June-July 1978, Vol. VII, No. 3; and October 1978, Vol. VII, No. 5.

——1979. 'Reports from Districts'. August 1979, vol. VIII, No. 5.

——1980. February-March, 1980, Vol. 9, No. 1, p. 38.

UNESCO 2002: LINK Project, International Council for Science and UNESCO, UNESCO, Geneva.

——2003. Text of the Convention for the Safeguarding of Intangible Cultural Heritage. Paris: UNESCO. Downloaded from *http://www.unesco.org/culture/ich/index.php?pg=2002*

Report of The United Nations Conference on Environment and Development, Rio de Janeiro, 3–14 June 1992. http://un.org/documents/ga/conf151/aconf15126-3.htm.

Plates

Plate No. 1: Siru Village

Plate No. 2: Paya Village

Plate No. 3: Water point at Siru

Plate No. 4: Investigator on the way to Siru

Plate No. 5: Jhum field, Bogo village

Plate No. 6: Sowing of paddy by dibbling method

Plate No. 7: Paper, logs to control Soil Erosion

Plate No. 8: Korti, used for weaving mats

Plate No. 9: Doka Putu, Lite Boje, believed to be the abode of yapoms

Plate No. 10: Hunting

Plate No. 11: Trapping

Plate No. 12: Seasoning Toko leaves to be used as thatching material

Plate No. 13: Tasum Kunam with Raju

Plate No. 14: Tasum/Tas Karnam

Plate No. 15: Takom Ganam

Plate No. 16: Lipum

Plate No. 17: Tanir (The bark used to stupefy fish)

Plate No. 18: Mute (Seeds used as herbal poison in hunting and fishing)

Plate No. 19: Preservation of Seeds

Plate No. 20: Ploughing and Levelling

Plate No. 21: Use of Pesticide

Plate No. 22: WRC fields at Tapo with Bamboo Plantations to prevent soil erosion

Plate No. 23: Water Canal for Irrigation constructed by the people at Kabu

Plate No. 24: Degraded Fishery Pond, Paya

Plate No. 25: New forms of Land Use Orange Garden with Toko plantations

Plate No. 26: Boulders Collected to be sold

Plate No. 27: A Jhum Plot at Tapo (July 2010)

Plate No. 28: A Jhum Plot at Kabu with commercial vegetables (February 2007)

Plate No. 29: Traditional Products for urban consumption in Aalo Bazar

Plate No. 30: Rural Production for Urban Consumption

Plate No. 31: Fire wood for sale

Plate No. 32: Transportation of Fire wood to Market

Index